Pilgrimage of Faith

Pilgrimage of Faith
Introducing the World Council of Churches

Donald W. Norwood

**World Council
of Churches**
Publications

Pilgrimage of Faith
Introducing the World Council of Churches

Donald W. Norwood
Edited by Kristine Greenaway

WCC Publications is the book publishing programme of the World Council of Churches. Founded in 1948, the WCC promotes Christian unity in faith, witness and service for a just and peaceful world. A global fellowship, the WCC brings together 348 Protestant, Orthodox, Anglican and other churches representing more than 550 million Christians in 110 countries and works cooperatively with the Roman Catholic Church.

Opinions expressed in WCC Publications are those of the authors.

Scripture quotations are from the New Revised Standard Version Bible, © copyright 1989 by the Division of Christian Education of the National Council of the Churches of Christ in the USA. Used by permission.

Cover design: Ellera Design
Book design and typesetting: Beth Oberholtzer
ISBN: 978-2-8254-1710-2

World Council of Churches
150 route de Ferney, P.O. Box 2100
1211 Geneva 2, Switzerland
http://publications.oikoumene.org

CONTENTS

FOREWORD

The story of the World Council of Churches is the story of encounters among our member churches. It is the story of praying, talking, and working together, of seeking to understand each other better in order to witness in unity to God's presence in the world. How appropriate it is then that this introduction to the WCC focuses on the ten great assemblies that have shaped our history over the past 70 years. Since the inaugural gathering in Amsterdam in 1948 through to the most recent assembly held in Busan, South Korea, in 2013, Christians from around the world have met every seven years to deliberate about the course the council should take in the years ahead.

As a global fellowship, we are alive to the pains, struggles, hopes, and joys of 550 million people connected to our 348 member churches. Together we seek to address social injustice, human rights abuses, destruction of the world's natural resources, and interfaith conflict. We seek too to engage with churches that are not WCC members, notably the Roman Catholic Church and most Pentecostal churches. As pilgrims seeking justice and peace, we are open to learning from each other and moving together, reinforced by our shared faith and deep commitment to God's call to be of service to our neighbours and good stewards of the earth.

Pilgrimage of Faith: Introducing the World Council of Churches is the third in a series of introductions to the WCC. In 1990 Marlin

VanElderen's *Introducing the World Council of Churches* appeared in WCC Publications' Risk Book Series. VanElderen's introduction was updated in a new edition that was revised and enlarged by Martin Conway in 2001. It is now Donald Norwood's turn to tell the story of the WCC. Norwood – a committed ecumenist with deep roots in the life of local parishes – understands how a global perspective can enrich congregational life when Christians are inspired by stories from the worldwide family of believers. As a journalist, Norwood knows how to engage us with frank and clear language and find the words to share the excitement and complexity of the evolving story of the WCC.

It is indeed a complex story with many dimensions and so we are grateful to Georges (Yorgo) Lemopoulos for reading the text and bringing to it the perspectives of Orthodox member churches. We are grateful as well that Mercy Oduyoye, a well known Kenyan Methodist theologian and ecumenist, has endorsed Norwood's approach to telling the story.

It is my hope that this introduction to the WCC will encourage you to become engaged in our common pilgrimage as we prepare for the next decades of joint action in celebration of God's presence in the world. There is a place for everyone in the worldwide family of WCC member churches. You are welcome!

Olav Fykse Tveit
General Secretary
World Council of Churches

WORLD CHURCH "COUNSELS"

What, Where, Why?

Now that I have finished the book I can tell you what it is about! It's about us – all 550 million of us who are members of the 348 member churches that form the World Council of Churches. The officers of the World Council of Churches are very busy people, visiting and organizing countless operations on our behalf. But the World Council is not just them; it's us. In our local congregations we carry out many tasks the World Council's officers support and encourage. But the policies they act on are those our representatives have agreed to when they meet in the assemblies. In each assembly we take counsel together, having first gathered together in worship and prayed for God's guidance. Hence my emphasis in this book is on taking "counsel" at the ten global assemblies of the World Council of Churches held since its formation in 1948.

Don't be put off by all this talk of councils, counsels, and committees – in addition to formal moments, they include informal conversations, much like a pilgrimage. One bonus of the pilgrimage round the island of Iona off the west coast of Scotland that my wife and I have often enjoyed is that you need not stay with the same person but can meet different people just by being together in a larger group and that you can slow down or speed up without appearing to be rude.

Where Is the WCC?

General Secretary Olav Fykse Tveit told the delegates at the 2013 assembly in Busan, South Korea, "The WCC is located wherever you are as member churches. You are the WCC."[1] The main offices are in the Ecumenical Centre in Geneva, conveniently located within walking distance of the city's international airport. But to emphasize the point that the WCC is a global body, its main decision-making body, the assembly, never meets in Geneva but has to date met in every continent. Each location also provides a specific context that has to be personally addressed, because as churches we care about each other where we are. What are the challenges we Christians face *together* because we are in Busan, South Korea, in a country torn in two by a war the middle-aged cannot even remember, or in Amsterdam 1948, soon after the war? So in this study I use each different location of an assembly to highlight issues which were often the dominant concerns of Christians in that place. At the same time, because each assembly brings together peoples from 110 nations, it has to deal with a whole range of issues that are not peculiar to one place but may affect us all. Racism and sexism are good examples. And so is unity. This is our *raison d'être*. Successive assemblies have attempted to describe "the unity we seek." This was first attempted at New Delhi in 1961 under the heading "all in each place."

The central committee, a body of some 150 representatives elected by the assembly to act as the WCC governing body between assemblies that does much of the planning and programming between assemblies, also meets in different locations. So does the Faith and Order commission, another important and foundational working commission of the WCC. Today, we are constantly reminded that most Christians live in the global South, so why not meet in Timbuktu?[2] The logistics and expense of travel often make Geneva the most convenient venue for smaller meetings. But we will always be sent on our way with the reminder the WCC is everywhere – where we are and also where we are needed most. The council's emphasis and guiding concept, and so the title of this book, is that we are all engaged in a *Pilgrimage of Faith*. This was the theme developed at the assembly in Busan. We join the pilgrimage wherever we are.

> WCC is everywhere – where we are and also where we are needed most.

Who and Where Am I?

Here I am in Oxford, England, Europe, and very conscious as I write of being part of the WCC. Three members of my Reformed congregation were active in the WCC and another an observer at Vatican II. It is thanks to them that I try to be ecumenical in all I do, say, and write. I have been helped in my global vision by attending assemblies and central committees for the last 20 years, as well as living in a very international city. In 2007–2008 my wife and I worked with students from all over the world who were studying at the WCC's Ecumenical Institute in Bossey, near Geneva. Through Facebook and emails, we are in regular contact with friends from Brazil to Beijing, and I am currently helping a student in India with his doctorate. It is now easier for many of us to say "the whole world is our parish" than it was for John Wesley when he made this claim in the 18th century. Wesley never had a mobile phone. Lucky man!

What Churches?

The WCC is a fellowship made up of national churches. In this it differs from the Roman Catholic Church, which is an international body bound together by obedience to the pope, who is also bishop of Rome. It has never been a purely Protestant body, but even in its early beginnings included Anglicans, who do not always like to be called Protestant, and Orthodox churches. In WCC's Faith and Order commission and some other projects, Roman Catholics are full members and have been since that great council, Vatican II (1962–1965), which committed the Church of Rome to participating in the global ecumenical movement, where it had previously been suspicious. The fact that it is organized internationally is one major reason why it would be difficult for the Church of Rome ever to become a member of the WCC as it is now structured. I shall explain later that we are exploring other options like the Global Christian Forum in the hope of broadening the spectrum to include Rome and also independent Evangelical and Pentecostal churches. This is a big issue. Half the world's Christians are Roman Catholics, and they can be found in almost every country. Another quarter of the world's Christians are Evangelical and Pentecostal, and in many parts of the world, including South America, these numbers are growing fast.

Why a World Council?

Even in New Testament times, Christians found it necessary and helpful to meet together with other Christians from other places. As recorded in Acts 15, they met together in Jerusalem to sort out one of the early problems of the relationship between Jewish and Gentile Christians. Though it brought together diverse followers of Jesus from different backgrounds, officially this meeting in Jerusalem is not listed as "the first ecumenical council." This title belongs to Nicaea in 325, which took place after things had developed further within the church. Most Christians recognize the first three such councils as part of their own history and tradition. The Eastern Orthodox count the first seven. Rome regards Vatican II as the 21st ecumenical council. What counts as an ecumenical council partly depends on how we define the term "ecumenical." Strictly speaking, but at the risk of being pedantic, the World Council of Churches is not a council. But then "United Nations" does not offer an accurate description of how things function in that organization either. The nations are not united but we wish they were; one purpose of gathering in a UN assembly is to bring nations together to resolve their differences and offer mutual support. The title of the World Council of Churches, too, reflects an aspiration churches are called to live up to. The fourth assembly of the WCC, meeting soon after Vatican II and inspired by its example of reaching out to other Christians, expressed the hope that one day there would be a general or ecumenical council that could speak for all Christians and pave the way into the future.[3] Father Cyrill Argenti, an Orthodox priest from France and main speaker at Nairobi, concluded his presentation with the wish that one of the WCC assemblies in the future be recognized as an ecumenical council.

Assemblies of the WCC are held every seven or eight years. The ecumenical councils were only convened when it was thought necessary. It is interesting that this was rarely only for church business. Emperor Constantine summoned the bishops to Nicaea. As the first Christian emperor, he was not a great theologian and was more concerned about the peace of the realm than sound doctrine; however, he could see that the Arian controversy was throwing parts of his empire into confusion, and so he summoned the council for the sake of peace. It is remembered to this day for its statement of faith, the Nicene Creed. Later councils of the church in the West were convened by the popes. They, too, might have had a concern for peace. Just why Pope John XXIII summoned Vatican II will always be something of a mystery. This prayerful man felt he was inspired by God to do so, but one of his interpreters, Norman Tanner, English editor of *Decrees of the Ecumenical Council*, in his own introduction to Vatican II, quotes Pope John XXIII's promulgation of the Second Vatican Council, "in which the pope publicly and officially summoned the council to meet in 1962 and stated three principal aims of the council, namely: the better internal ordering of the church, unity among Christians, and the promotion of peace throughout the world."[4] The pope, like all the bishops at the council, had lived through and survived the Second World War. They were now enduring the Cold War and feared a third world war following the Cuban Missile Crisis of October 1962, taking place just as the council began. Peace had to be on the agenda. And so it was for the first WCC assembly at Amsterdam in 1948, as well on the agenda of all other assemblies that followed. Those who criticize the WCC for being more concerned about justice and peace than the unity of the church need to be reminded that there are good precedents. Council agendas were rarely confined to church business. On the other hand, it is fair and necessary to remind the WCC of its divine mandate as stated in the Constitution: "The primary purpose of the fellowship of churches in the World Council of Churches is to call one another to visible unity in one faith and one Eucharistic fellowship, expressed in worship and in common life in Christ, through witness and service to the world, and to advance towards that unity in order that the world may believe."[5] So stated, the Constitution may be best understood as a commentary on Jesus' prayer in John 17:21, that all may be one that the world may believe.

The Bible is basic for the ecumenical movement. There we read not only of the Council at Jerusalem but also of Paul's missionary journeys and visits to different churches and the collection he raised among Gentile congregations for the poor in Jerusalem. This, too, provides a precedent for why we need a global coordinating body like a World Council. Paul's collection sets an example of what came to be known soon after the Second World War as the Inter-Church Aid and Refugee Service. His pastoral care for different congregations as reflected in most of his letters sets the pattern for visits to member churches by the WCC general secretary and for teams of people appointed by the WCC to act as living letters (2 Cor. 3:2–3) when they meet with churches in troubled places and offer the support and solidarity of the wider fellowship. A good example of a pilgrimage of faith.

This study focuses on assemblies, but it is important to remember that what each assembly brings to the delegates is the result of what the WCC's governing bodies have carefully considered and decided and what the WCC programmes have been doing since last they met. One vital way we can all join in is through prayer. Jesus' prayer for the coming kingdom bids us embrace the whole world and its churches. Many of us use the Ecumenical Prayer Cycle, prepared and published by the WCC, and, week by week, in our local congregation, pray for every country and every church, in turn.

Why Not?

Answering why, where, and what questions could easily become a defence of the status quo. The World Council of Churches, like its member churches, is in constant need of reform, and at its best admits this. That is why in a final chapter I explore some of the issues raised by young theologians from different continents who were invited to offer "Proposals for Ecumenism in the Twenty-First Century," and why I describe experiments with new structures such as the Global Christian Forum. I will also revisit the question that popular popes like John XXIII and Francis provoke, namely: "Could there be a 'pope for all Christians'?" Today's global media loves a good pope, whereas it cannot cope with a good council, Vatican II notwithstanding.

People or Places, Topics or Towns?

Readers of this book may easily be confused because I do not report everything that happened everywhere the WCC met. This is because I am trying to demonstrate how relevant the WCC was in the past and is for our Christian life, here and now. To do this, I select ten major issues dealt with in ten assemblies. Each assembly discussed many more topics, some of them frankly boring. If you were a delegate you might like people to know that you were elected to one of the key committees or how much your church pays, but if not, who cares?

At the start of each chapter I shall offer a brief introduction to that assembly but then select one or two key themes that 70 years later remain significant landmarks in our ecumenical pilgrimage of faith. Most of the big themes were dealt with in more than one assembly. Does the place where these discussions are held matter? I went to Brazil in 2006 but saw very little of Brazil. It was still important to be there, not least to show that we, the world church, care about Brazil and have read about it and prayed for it. Pilgrims on a journey press on because of the welcome and hospitality they receive from strangers. In the ecumenical movement we move on to different places because of encouragement from people in Porto Alegre, Harare, and Busan, who were so glad we came, through our representatives. Many have lived through tough times and, thanks to our visit, no longer feel alone. Notice how important hospitality is for God's pilgrim people in Bible lands. The kindness of strangers is never to be taken for granted as we journey on from place to place, project to project, never finally at home anywhere except at last in heaven, but even now in Christ with his different disciples.

Tomorrow?

I am very conscious that everything I write becomes dated the moment it is written. A remedy is close at hand on our laptops, phones, and iPads. The WCC provides almost daily online information on its activities. Its quarterly journal *The Ecumenical Review* is accessible online and will keep you well informed on current thinking, usually with a specific concern for each issue. The Ecumenical Prayer Cycle – in both its print edition, *Pilgrim Prayer: The Ecumenical Prayer Cycle,* and its weekly posting of prayers – can be read in relation to weekly bulletins from the WCC where the council's response to issues facing different regions of the world are highlighted. Compare what you read in this global publication with the prayers in your local congregation before you say "Amen" too quickly. Too often we act and pray as though our church is the only church. We pray for the world but not for the world church. Roman Catholics always pray for the pope. Let us pray for the pope, for all heads of churches, all Christian communities, *and* the World Council of Churches. They need our prayers, and prayers should be well informed. May this book help you to pray.

CHAPTER ONE

AMSTERDAM 1948

"Man's Disorder and God's Design"

Each assembly has a comprehensive theme. It is usually chosen by members of the central committee that guides the WCC in between assemblies, and the choice reflects current concerns, which it is hoped will excite and get congregations everywhere thinking about their faith. Eleven years had passed since it was decided to have a World Council, and a lot had happened in the world since 1937. The provisional committee had no difficulty in describing what the whole world had experienced: "Man's Disorder." They met in 1946 only months after the war ended and, by the time the assembly met, had prepared four volumes of essays on different aspects, each with a focus on the church: the Universal Church in God's Design; the Church's Witness to God's Design; the Church and Society; and the Church and the International Disorder. Possibly no assembly was better prepared, but a single assembly could not tackle such a vast agenda. It did not.

Church and World after Two World Wars

The crowds who gathered in the streets of Amsterdam in August 1948 witnessed a miracle of God's victorious ruling. Only a few years earlier they were forced to watch Nazi troops stamping through their towns and hounding their homes. A young Jewish girl, Anne Frank, and her family were in hiding, hoping every hour that no one would betray them and dispatch them to Auschwitz. Their much-loved Queen, Wilhelmina, had to hide for her own safety, and had been bitterly disappointed in the war years that when the churches were most needed, they were most divided. Her fellow countryman, Willem Visser 't Hooft, had tried hard to persuade her then that new life had come to the churches.[1] She hoped so. And now here in Amsterdam 1948, Christians were coming together, as never before, even round the Lord's own table, though not all felt able to celebrate together. In the opening worship in the stately Nieuwe Kirk, the Orb and Cross of Christ surmounted the crown of all earthly royalties, affirming that it is Christ and Christ alone who is the sovereign Lord of all, in the church and in the world – something that Hitler and his supporters had tried in vain to deny. The Thousand-Year Reich had expired after little more than a decade, but at massive cost.

It was not hard to choose a theme for this assembly, but it was easy to get it the wrong way round. If we start with humanity's disorder and the mess we have made of the world, we Christians end up sounding just as depressed and hopeless as the rest of the world. The theologian Karl Barth and other participants soon made it clear that, as Christians, all our thinking must begin with God, with thankfulness and praise to God for what he has done and is doing in Christ. It is only in the light of God's design and kingdom, not ours, that with his help we can tackle

. . . here in Amsterdam 1948, Christians were coming together, as never before . . .

the world's and the church's disorder. These were the convictions widely shared in the opening worship and speeches at this pioneer assembly. They are recorded in the assembly report, edited by the first general secretary of the WCC, Willem Visser 't Hooft.

The people who took part in this first assembly brought their own personal testimonies to the central themes of our Christian faith: forgiveness and reconciliation, God's sovereign rule over the nations, the experience of our God-given unity in Christ. Martin Niemöller and Bishop Otto Dibelius had survived the Hitler years in Germany partly because of international ecumenical support from other churches in other lands. They had made their public confession and been reconciled to their former enemies at Stuttgart soon after the war ended. Bishop George Bell of Chichester, as a good prophet, was not without honour save in his own country, where he was often unpopular as an outspoken critic of the policy of saturation bombing of German cities and civilians.[2] He might also see himself as representing Dietrich Bonhoeffer, destined to play a leading role in the World Council had he not been executed on Hitler's orders just as the war was ending. Another bishop, Berggrav of Norway, had experienced unity when, while under house arrest, he was informed that Archbishop William Temple in England was praying for him. Then I knew, he said, that the church is one! Temple was not present to witness all this. He died in 1944, but England's most quoted archbishop will always be remembered for saying at his inauguration that this worldwide Christian fellowship, this ecumenical movement, is "the great new fact of our era." John Foster Dulles, secretary of state to President Eisenhower of the United States, might have been spotted beside theologian Josef Hromadka of Czechoslovakia before this assembly. If so, that was another miracle, for in the assembly debates the two men would clash

> ... this ecumenical movement, is "the great new fact of our era."

over whether the World Council of Churches (WCC) should stand up for so-called Western Christian values and oppose atheistic communism, or offer support to people like Hromadka, who believed it was their Christian vocation to witness to Christ wherever one happened to live. This debate took place following a meeting in Moscow that had condemned the WCC and severely criticized it for promoting exclusively Western values. A future clash was not yet in evidence. Soon a Chinese delegate, Professor T.C. Chao, would resign from the central committee, the governing body that meets between assemblies, because he disagreed with policy statements about the war in Korea. Almost at the same time, Christian missionaries were being forced out of China as part of Mao's revolution; the church in China that today is growing rapidly became for decades an underground movement, no longer in contact with the WCC until it was welcomed back at the assembly in Canberra in 1991. Only God could bring such a diverse gathering of people together after the trauma of world war. He did! The assembly declared its wish to "stay together" and for the most part has succeeded, though not without painful struggles.

As well as the overall theme, the date and place (Europe) would shape much of the agenda. What did the council have to say about war, about the United Nations organization that had replaced the League of Nations, which had failed so miserably to prevent another war, and about human rights? One million people were displaced from their homes and homelands because of the war. Alas, in 2018 there are more than 60 million refugees! Today, as the European community and the United Nations struggle to reach agreement as to how best to cope, churches recall their sacred texts about care for the aliens and strangers within their gates. Care for the refugee and asylum seeker remains another of those big concerns that can never be resolved by one generation, much less one assembly, because new conflicts go on adding to their numbers. But first there were two agenda items the WCC needed to discuss at this first assembly, because they would shape its future work:

1. the nature of the WCC: what it is and what it is not; and
2. the authority of WCC assemblies and WCC pronouncements on world affairs.

What the WCC Is and What It Is Not

At Amsterdam, Visser 't Hooft asked and answered this question:

> What then is the function of our Council? Our name gives us a clue to an answer. We are a Council of Churches, not *the* Council of the one undivided Church. Our name indicates our weakness and our shame before God, for there can be and there *is* only one Church of Christ on earth. Our plurality is a deep anomaly. But our name indicates also that we are aware of that situation, that we do not accept it passively, that we would move forward to the manifestation of the One Holy Church. Our Council represents therefore an emergency solution – a stage on the road – a body living between the time of complete isolation of the churches from each other and the time – on earth or in heaven – when it will be visibly true that there is one Shepherd and one flock.[3]

In much of what he said, he could be quoting his friend and fellow Reformed churchman Karl Barth. Barth prepared a lecture for the Faith and Order conference that met at Edinburgh in 1937 which, together with the Life and Work committee in Oxford that same summer in that same year, made the decision to form a World Council of Churches. Barth had said, "We have no right to explain the multiplicity of the churches at all. We have to deal with it as we deal with sin, our own and others, as guilt which we must take upon ourselves, to recognise it as a fact, to understand it as the impossible thing which has intruded itself. . . . If Christ is indeed the unity of the Church, then the only multiplicity which can be normal is that *within* the Church."[4]

On the other hand, Visser 't Hooft would realize that his understanding of the ecumenical task was not shared by the Church of Rome. Rome at this stage would have nothing to do with the WCC and would not allow representation at Amsterdam 1948 or Evanston 1954, though it was becoming interested enough to send four observers to the Lund Faith and Order conference in 1952. In Rome's official view, the church is *already* one. It has one earthly shepherd, the pope, as successor of Peter, commissioned by Jesus to feed his flock (John 21:15–17). Rome could and would shortly convene a council and regard it as a council of the whole church, an ecumenical council, not a council of different and separate churches. Visser 't Hooft is agreeing with Rome that there can only be one church. He is disagreeing that this one church already exists: the Church of Rome. And Rome, partly in response to the ecumenical movement beyond her borders, would modify her own claims. At Vatican II (1962–1965), she no longer says we are the one and only church. We are still, for the time being, the best expression of the one, holy, catholic, and apostolic church confessed in the Creed: "this church, set up and organized in this world as a society, subsists in the catholic church, governed by the successor of Peter and the bishops in communion with him."[5] The shift in emphasis from *is* to *subsists* is subtle – so subtle that some deny there had been any change! There had. At the Second Vatican Council, Rome committed herself to join in the ecumenical movement, thus admitting there is more to being the one church of God than what Rome on her own manifests. The decision was ratified by Pope John Paul II in his Ecumenical Encyclical *Ut Unum Sint* in 1995. Such ecumenical commitment is a great step forward, for half the world's Christians are not Roman Catholic.

This fundamental ecclesiological question was debated by the Eastern Orthodox churches in a council held in Crete in 2016, where the dilemma between "being the one, holy, catholic and apostolic church" and "relating to other Christian churches" or "becoming a member of ecumenical church organizations" was one of the burning issues.

Constitution and Further Reflection

Years before Vatican II, ecumenically minded Roman Catholics like Yves Congar, a French Dominican friar, priest, and theologian and an early advocate of ecumenism, met secretly with representatives of the WCC. One point to be clarified was what the WCC was. What was it called to do? The Constitution agreed at Amsterdam set forth six functions:

1. to carry on the work of Faith and Order and Life and Work to facilitate common action by the churches,

2. to promote co-operation in study,

3. to promote the growth of ecumenical consciousness in the members of all the churches,

4. to establish relations with denominational federations and other ecumenical movements,

5. to call world conferences on specific subjects as occasion may require, and

6. to support the churches in their work of evangelism.[6]

There was clearly a need for further reflection and clarification: this task was undertaken by the central committee meeting in Toronto in 1950, which agreed on the document *The Church, the Churches and the World Council of Churches*. Its main points about the WCC are these:

1. The World Council of Churches is not and must never become a super-church. It cannot act or legislate for its member churches.

2. The purpose of the World Council of Churches is to bring the churches into living contact with each other and to promote the study and discussion of the issues of church unity.

3. Membership in the World Council does not imply the acceptance of a specific doctrine concerning the nature of church unity.

4. Membership does not imply that each church must regard the other member churches as churches in the true and full sense of the word.

The WCC report *The First Six Years, 1948–1954,* which was prepared for the next assembly at Evanston, reported that the statement about the ecclesiological significance of the World Council had received "sufficiently numerous" responses from member churches to assure delegates that the Toronto Declaration was an acceptable basis for future work. That may now seem surprising, as nearly 70 years later the ecclesiological significance of the WCC is an unresolved issue. When Christians of different traditions and countries come together, they may have a richer experience of being the church catholic than they ever do back home, in their own congregations; yet according to current theological understanding, their meeting together is not church. What then is it? No one seems to know! The Scottish Presbyterian missionary Lesslie Newbigin (1909–1998) suggested in 1960 that the WCC is provisionally "a form of being-together in Christ."[7] It is proving quite difficult to move on beyond the rather tentative and cautious statements agreed in Toronto in 1950. In 1989, a process was initiated which even in its title admits we are trying to move on but are not sure how: *Towards a Common Understanding and Vision of the World Council of Churches.* It tells us that "the description of the WCC as a 'fellowship of churches' indicates clearly that the Council is not itself a church," but it goes on to comment that since many of us describe our own congregations and church gatherings as fellowships, "the use of the term in the Basis of the WCC does suggest that the Council is more than a mere functional association of churches set up to organise activities in areas of common interest." What we experience in the WCC and in other ecumenical meetings is some form, however imprecise and imperfect, of our *koinonia* in Christ, using a key word in the Greek of the New Testament which cannot easily be translated by one word in English, since it means communion, community, sharing, and participation – all of which are aspects of our life together in Christ. The *Common Understanding* statement was sent to member churches for comment and then accepted by WCC's jubilee assembly at Harare in 1998.

One is tempted to apologize for what may appear to be theological quibbles about what the WCC is or is not. The issue is, however, important, for it makes a world of difference to the authority and influence the WCC may exercise in world affairs. Is it just a body of ecumenically minded women and men who enjoy meeting together from time to time for a good discussion, or do its decisions have behind them real churchly authority? Rome, either through the pope or through a council, speaks with authority. Can the World Council sometimes speak authoritatively for the 348 member churches and for the 550 million Christians who are represented by delegates at assemblies and central committee meetings? This question was also on the Amsterdam agenda, and was answered in the light of experience in the following years.

Assemblies' Authority

1. The authority of official WCC pronouncements is only the authority of the truth they contain.

2. As agreed at Amsterdam, statements by the WCC are not binding on any church unless that church has confirmed them and made them on its own.

3. The Council should only issue pronouncements on issues which affect the life of many churches or the whole world.

4. Pronouncements must have the backing of a "substantial conviction" within the constituency of the council though there should also be a place for minority views and prophetic leadership.

5. The World Council should avoid identifying itself with any particular political, racial, or social interests.[8]

The Toronto Statement undergirds all that is said here with a more explicit theological basis. "Since the very *raison d'être* of the Church is to witness to Christ, churches cannot meet together without seeking from their common Lord a common witness before the world. This will not always be possible. But when it proves possible thus to speak or act together, the churches can gratefully accept it as God's gracious gift that in spite of their disunity, he has enabled them to render one and the same witness, and that they may thus manifest something of the unity, the purpose of which is precisely 'that the world may believe' (John 17:21)."

At Amsterdam we see the churches trying hard to think theologically in their address to the wider world. So they declared: "War as a method of settling disputes is incompatible with the teaching and example of our Lord Jesus Christ. The part which war plays in our present international life is a sin against God and a degradation of man." In the same paragraph they went on to query whether the Christian Just War tradition was now outmoded in an era of atomic war and the possibilities of total destruction.[9] Member churches and individual Christians might not agree, but after a world war and the dropping of atomic bombs on Hiroshima and Nagasaki, everyone is entitled to ask, "What has the Christian church to say?"

Sometimes the member churches urged the council to do some theology and not simply repeat what any well-meaning person might think. Women in the member churches want to hear if the council has anything distinctive to say about the man–woman relationship as well as about the life and work of women in the church.[10]

Like all the big issues discussed in this book, we have to go on asking questions about what the church or the churches say and how they say it. Early on in the WCC's history, US theologian Paul Ramsey wrote a critique of the WCC Geneva Conference on Church and Society 1966 with the title *Who Speaks for the Church?*[11] He prefers to see the churches encouraging open, responsible discussion of various options rather than appearing to know best what is the one and only right thing to do. On the other side, fellow US theologian Robert McAfee Brown, an active WCC participant, was quite sure that the war in Vietnam and the way it was being waged was absolutely wrong, and said so. He could quote support from statements by the WCC central committee, the National Council of Churches in America, the Synagogue Council of America, and an Encyclical by Pope Paul VI, *Christi Matri*.[12] In the free and open debate that Paul Ramsey advocates, one would need to be a very good theologian to refute the counsels of so many councils. Christian discernment includes respect for the wisdom of other Christians.

More recently, Keith Clements, a Baptist theologian in WCC's Faith and Order commission and one-time secretary of the Conference of European Churches, returned to the same topic with his *Learning to Speak: The Church's Voice in Public Affairs*.[13] One of his key points is that the church is not necessarily best qualified to teach the world how to live. It needs to be a better listener.

From Principles to Policies

Each assembly sets much of the agenda that the central committee and related bodies work out until the following assembly. In Amsterdam, member churches were asked to help clarify "the ecclesiological significance" of the World Council of Churches and did so, as we have seen, in sufficient numbers to assure a working agreement. In turn, suggestions were put to the member churches.

In its *Word to the Churches*, the Faith and Order conference at Lund (1952) said: "We have been sent to Lund by our Churches to study together what measure of unity in matters of faith, church order and worship exists among our Churches and how we may move forward towards the fuller unity God wills for us." They then put questions to the churches that had sent them: "We would, therefore, earnestly request our Churches to consider whether they are doing all they ought to do to manifest the oneness of the people of God. Should not our Churches ask themselves whether they are showing sufficient eagerness to enter into conversation with other Churches and whether they should not act together in all matters except those in which deep differences of conviction compel them to act separately."[14]

The first part of the statement follows on from what was said at Toronto – that it is not the task of the World Council of Churches "to negotiate unions between churches, which can only be done by the churches themselves." Whether it was due to encouragement from this WCC conference or not, many churches did in fact enter into dialogues with other churches, even if they took their time to do so. Apart from the Bonn Agreement between the Old Catholics and the Church of England in 1931, all the conversations listed in the first WCC volume of dialogues, *Growth in Agreement*, date from the 1970s.[15] There are now two further volumes. Prior to the formation of the WCC, some churches had united to form one church in Canada as the United Church of Canada (1925), and in India as the Church of South India (1947).

"Should not our Churches ask themselves . . . whether they should not act together in all matters except those in which deep differences of conviction compel them to act separately."

And by way of advice and not just encouragement, our "experts" at Lund tell us that it is no longer helpful only to compare notes about how different churches do different things. It is better instead to search for common ground, or as would be later stated in *Baptism, Eucharist and Ministry* (1982) and *The Church: Towards a Common Vision* (2013), to discover many "convergences" that then assure us that "despite much diversity in theological expression the churches have much in common in their understanding of the faith."[16] Even in personal conversations with Christians from other traditions, we can quickly discover that there are more things that unite us than divide us, but too often we concentrate on the disagreements and differences. Karl Barth often recalled a conversation he had with a Roman Catholic who told him: "Don't let's talk about the pope. Let's talk about Christ!" Then, said Barth, the real dialogue began.

The challenge to do as much as we can together remains. We have a great deal of potential to do a lot of our thinking together, about the faith and about various ethical issues, in WCC meetings, and to be helped by the documents they issue. We can act together, as its name implies, through the ecumenical emergency relief and development network ACT Alliance, and through other Christian aid agencies, like the Roman Catholic organizations CAFOD and Caritas, or the Evangelical TEAR Fund (though admittedly, different convictions about contraception may still prompt such agencies to act separately). Despite opportunities to work together, churches are still inclined to go it alone unless strapped for cash. And today they are. This could be read as one blessing coming out of common difficulties: the increasing struggle to find adequate funding is requiring churches and faith-based organizations to find more creative ways of working together.

For the British general election of 2015, there could have been but there was not a jointly prepared document voicing common Christian concerns about poverty, people with disabilities, relations with Europe, the Trident nuclear deterrent renewal, etc. Even a document that admitted our disagreements would witness to the fact that we are now listening to each other, are united in our concern for the common good, and are ready to share in debate.

Amsterdam and its follow-up meetings also helped member churches clarify their response to political issues and world affairs. Churches are scolded for being too political, yet it has never been possible to avoid politics – and indeed, prior to the Western Enlightenment, many peoples would not have understood our modern distinctions between religion and politics. The question is how we respond to world events. Amsterdam came up with two suggestions. The first was that it was vital to create a fellowship of churches from different sides of the so-called Iron Curtain that in Germany became the Berlin Wall. The second applies to us all: "Man is created and called to be a free being, responsible to God and his neighbour." Wherever we are, Christians should encourage the growth of "the responsible society," one "where those who hold political authority

Selecting Delegates

Each member church appointed its own delegates to the assembly partly based on a quota system according to the membership of a particular church. Later attempts would be made to achieve a more balanced representation of ordained and lay, women and men, youth delegates and people with different disabilities. This in turn poses a challenge to member churches which give less scope for women's leadership or make few provisions for people who may, for example, be hearing impaired but have much to contribute to any church.

or economic power are responsible for its exercise to God and the people whose welfare is affected by it."[17] Such a guideline would be further elaborated at the next assembly, held at Evanston in 1954.

As mentioned earlier, the wider issue was the subject of the clash between US secretary of state Foster Dulles and the Czech professor Josef Hromadka. Is it the task of the WCC to uphold Western Christian values against atheistic communism, or can it help all its member churches minister wherever they happen to be? If some Christians find it possible to be Christians and capitalists, can we understand and work with and pray with those who find it possible to be Christians and communists? In the debates at Amsterdam and in subsequent discussion, the WCC made it clear that it is not a party to the East–West, Cold War conflict. There are good Christian women and men on both sides of the Iron Curtain, and the church refuses to recognize this border. Delegates at Lund must have felt rather ashamed when Hromadka told them, "I have had a rather depressing experience that my not unprovocative dogmatic heresies would be tolerated, overlooked or leniently listened to, whereas my Christian loyalty . . . has been questioned on account of my political and social point of view and decision."[18]

The whole debate at Amsterdam in 1948 might have been helped by the detailed study published in 1958 by the assistant director of the WCC's Institute at Bossey, Charles West. His doctoral thesis, on "Communism and the Theologians," dealt in detail with Swiss theologian Emil Brunner, who supported the Foster Dulles' line, and Barth, who was much closer to Hromadka.[19] West also commented on the views of Reinhold Niebuhr and Paul Tillich. We may think now, post-1989 when the Berlin Wall was dismantled, that the whole study was overtaken by events following that momentous change, but when the book was published, it would have been useful background reading for all who were caught up in the East–West conflict. The balanced stance of the WCC made it possible for the

Russian Orthodox Church to join the World Council at New Delhi in 1961, as well as for other Orthodox churches, like the Church of Georgia, to follow suit. But state officials often did their best to prevent the "two sides" from meeting. Trying to be fair to both sides is never easy, and the WCC has often been criticized for being soft on Soviet injustices while being harsher in its criticism of colonial powers or the practice of apartheid. And critics asked Barth why he opposed Nazism with such vigour, but not communism. His answer would not please everyone. He did not see communism as a threat to the Christian faith. Nazism was.

After Amsterdam and the Matter of Participants

As noted in the introduction, I am not attempting in this and subsequent chapters to do justice to all the matters dealt with in one assembly. Here I have highlighted some issues which in retrospect we can see were of lasting importance.

One other observation needs comment. Had you been at Amsterdam, Toronto, or Lund, you would be most impressed by the calibre of the men, but alas they were nearly all men, and the women who were present were a small minority. Thank God that the gospel has been revealed to babes in arms, but our Christian faith can and should still engage some of the best minds. The pioneers of the WCC were not fools. They included some of the best minds of their generation. The same was also true of those who advised the Roman Catholic council 20 years later.

Barth and C.H. Dodd gave keynote addresses at Amsterdam. Barth is still recognized as one of the greatest theologians of the 20th century – the greatest, according to Pope Pius XII, since Aquinas. Dodd was one of the leading New Testament scholars, and future director of the New English Bible project. An older generation will still revere Nicholas Zernov, John Baillie, Leonard Hodgson, Alex Vidler, and

George Florovsky. In preparatory papers for the assembly, who could tap into the wisdom of Tillich, Brunner, Niebuhr, and Bennett. And though there are too few women involved, they are very remarkable people: Sarah Chakko, Kathleen Bliss, Madeleine Barot, Suzanne de Dietrich, and Henriette Visser 't Hooft. Earlier meetings, such as Life and Work in Oxford in 1937, had engaged renowned professors like Sir Alfred Zimmern, Max Huber, and Ernest Barker. Looking back rather nostalgically, it is easy to say "there were giants in those days." Indeed there were! We can be thankful. We have no need to be envious. It is not our task to judge. We can build on their legacy.

Each assembly sends a message to the churches. If churches respond, it will be read out in each congregation, at least in summary. One phrase from the Message from Amsterdam has often been repeated, because subsequent generations feel duty bound to honour its pledge to "stay together," the determination of our founding fathers and mothers. One of these pioneers, Kathleen Bliss, wrote this crucial sentence: "Here in Amsterdam we have committed ourselves afresh to Christ and have covenanted with one another in constituting this World Council of Churches. We intend to stay together." As pilgrims, we must continue the journey they faithfully began. Harare repeated the phrase, but Busan, with its emphasis on pilgrimage, encourages us not just to stay together, but to move on to both deeper action and deeper conversation.

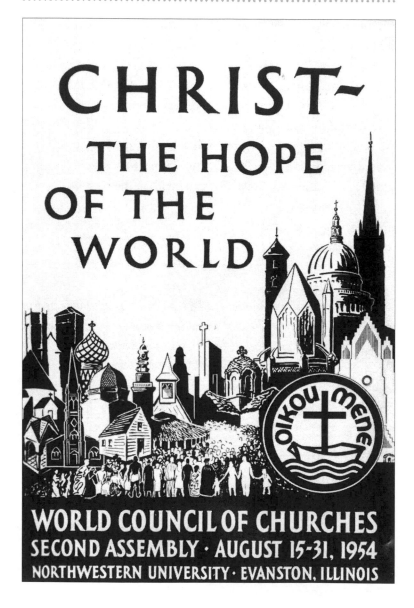

CHRIST -
THE HOPE OF THE WORLD

WORLD COUNCIL OF CHURCHES
SECOND ASSEMBLY · AUGUST 15-31, 1954
NORTHWESTERN UNIVERSITY · EVANSTON, ILLINOIS

CHAPTER TWO

EVANSTON 1954

"Christ – The Hope of the World"

People still go on pilgrimages to Santiago de Compostela centuries after this city in Spain became the shrine of St James. The pilgrims start from different places and are offered hospitality in different towns and villages along the way. So it is, and was, with those determined to stay together after Amsterdam. They set their sights on gathering in Evanston in the mid-western area of the United States of America. Why Evanston?

The short answer is because member churches in the United States invited them. Evanston, near Chicago, had the facilities to host the pilgrims whose numbers had grown, and have grown, every year they journey on. The World Council of Churches was on the way to becoming a global movement. Despite holding key events in Edinburgh in 1910, Stockholm in 1925, and Lausanne in 1937, and having its offices in Geneva, the ecumenical movement has never been a European affair. Some of its key players, like Bishop Charles Brent and John R. Mott, came from the United States, and the Orthodox theologian Father George Florovsky worked there from 1949 to 1979. All had been active in different ways in the ecumenical movement for years. Brent, who became bishop of western New York in 1917, died in 1929, but Mott, the great Methodist student leader and evangelist, took part in the Life and Work Conference in Stockholm in 1925, Faith and Order conferences in Lausanne 1927 and Edinburgh 1937, and was fit enough, then aged 82, to preach the sermon at Amsterdam in 1948. Mott died in Evanston shortly after the assembly met in his hometown. He did not live to see his younger US contemporary, Eugene Carson Blake, succeed the Dutchman Willem Visser 't Hooft as general secretary of the WCC in 1966. Florovsky, who took part in discussions leading to the Toronto Statement, was a long-time ecumenist of the Orthodox diaspora. So many who journeyed to Evanston in 1954 would be greeted by ecumenical friends they had come to love and respect over many years. They had much to discuss; I select only a few key themes.

The Hope of Israel and the People of God

When the member churches of the World Council of Churches assembled for the first time in 1948, it was obvious that we would need to think about the church, the churches, and the nature of such a council. Equally obvious, but for different though related reasons, our delegates would have to think about the Jews. They began to do this at Amsterdam, and at Evanston six years later tried to relate Israel's hopes to the main theme of "Christ – the Hope of the World." This proved too difficult for most members of the assembly. In theory, the link is obvious once you admit that Jesus was a Jew. Even Luther had said this. But a lot had happened since Luther, some of it because of Luther's later rash remarks about the Jews; much of it was in the living memory of those who were now

representing the churches of Europe and North America. Since the
conferences at Oxford and at Edinburgh in 1937, when the agreement to form a council had been reached, six million Jews had
been murdered in Europe. A Jewish state had been established in
Palestine. What did the churches have to say? Later, in 1962 to
1965, when Roman Catholics met in council, the Dominican Yves
Congar wrote, "Twenty years after Auschwitz it is impossible that
the Church should say nothing."[1]

Alas, it had been all too easy to say nothing. When Protestant
Christians in Germany, from Lutheran, Reformed, and United
Churches, met together at Barmen in 1934, they issued strong
words about obedience to Jesus but they never mentioned the Jews.
After the war, leaders of the churches in Germany pleaded to be
invited back into the ecumenical fold, and at Stuttgart made a stir-
ring confession of guilt that still moves us by its eloquence, even
in translation: "Through us has endless suffering been brought to
many peoples and countries. We accuse ourselves for not witnessing
more courageously, for not praying more faithfully, for not believing more joyously and for not loving more ardently."[2] To such honest admissions of failure most of us could say, "Amen, we too!"
But at Stuttgart in October 1945, so soon after the Holocaust, they
never mentioned the Jews. When Wolfgang Gerlach wrote a doctoral thesis entitled *The Confessing Church and the Persecution of the Jews*
in Germany, he had to wait another 20 years before anyone would
publish a work that exposed the failures of some contemporary
church leaders to speak out.[3] It's easy to be critical. But whenever
I am tempted to sound even more self-righteous, I am chastened
by the wise words of one of our best historians of the Nazi era, Ian
Kershaw: "I should like to think that had I been around at the time
I would have been a convinced anti-Nazi engaged in the underground resistance fight. However, I know really that I would have

. . . we can now see more clearly what questions we all need to ask when we think about Christians and Jews . . .

been as confused, and felt as helpless, as most of the people I am writing about."[4]

The truth is, most Christians in Europe, not just in Germany, were confused. They did not know what to make of Hitler's support for "Positive Christianity." One would need to be a very perceptive theologian to realize back in 1933 that what Hitler was hinting at was a total rewriting of the whole Bible and the Christian faith. Banish the Old Testament. Silence Paul and all soft talk of love of enemies. Even Martin Niemöller and Bishop Otto Dibelius had once been taken in, and both were now active in the WCC, having admitted they had been terribly wrong, or too easily misled. Now, thanks to their input, and thanks to insights and years of hard thinking by members of the worldwide church, not just in the World Council, but also among Roman Catholics after Vatican II, we are, or can be, better informed. It is also some consolation for us Christians to learn that some Jews, like Nahum Goldman and Irving Greenberg, blame themselves for being too easily deceived by Hitler, for being overly optimistic about human progress, and for believing that such an evil regime would not last.[5] At least we can now see more clearly what questions we all need to ask when we think about Christians and Jews, about the church and Israel, about the laity and the people of God. Let's look at some of the questions all Christians and their churches ought to ask and see what help is offered to us and our churches by the World Council of Churches' assemblies, commissions, and committees, by some member churches, by the Second Vatican Council, and by Jews themselves.

Important questions to raise include the following:

1. Jesus was a Jew. What difference does this make to our attitude to other Jews?

2. Do we just talk about Jews or [do we] converse with Jews?
3. Was the Holocaust our fault?
4. Has the New Testament replaced the Old?
5. What is our favourite biblical image of the church: e.g., bride of Christ, body of Christ, people of God? What difference does our preference make?
6. Are Jews the objects of mission or the subjects of dialogue?
7. If we criticize the policies of the State of Israel, does this make us anti-Semitic?

Are Jews the Objects of Mission or the Subjects of Dialogue?

Prior to the formation of the WCC, the International Missionary Council's emphasis was on mission to the Jews. A committee report titled "Concerns of the Churches" presented at Amsterdam acknowledged that "we have failed to fight with all our strength the age-old disorder of man which anti-Semitism represents" and admits that in the past, churches "have helped foster an image of the Jews as the sole enemies of Christ." It then urges the churches to engage more fully in mission to the Jews while admitting that it may be difficult for Christians to convince Jews that we have their welfare at heart. Indeed it might, after colluding with, or doing too little to stop, the murder of six million Jews! But Amsterdam only hints at mistreatment, not at murder. Helmut Gollwitzer, who had been Niemöller's colleague and later successor in Berlin during the Nazi era, argued that because of the way Christians had treated the Jews, they had forfeited the right to evangelize the Jews. In England, the Anglican theologian James Parkes, pioneer of Christian Jewish relations, said in 1969, "We have failed to convert the Jews and we shall always fail because it is not God's will."[6]

Was the Holocaust Our Fault as Christian People?

Amsterdam did not apologize. Nor did Vatican II. The assembly held in New Delhi in 1961 did. They affirmed that what the churches taught was wrong and stated, "In Christian teaching the historic events which led to the crucifixion should not be so presented as to fasten on the Jewish people of today responsibilities which belong to our corporate humanity and not to one race or community. Jews were the first to accept Jesus and Jews are not the only ones who do not recognise him."[7]

Such a statement was warmly welcomed by Cardinal Bea and quoted with approval by the *Jewish Chronicle*.[8] Bea, secretary for Christian Unity, hoped that the Second Vatican Council might say the same. It did not, and for this was roundly rebuked by Karl Barth in his comments on the council document *Nostra Aetate*: "Would it not be more appropriate, in view of the anti-Semitism of the ancient, the medieval and to a large degree the modern church, to set forth an explicit confession of guilt here?"[9] Indeed it would! But the council did make it quite clear that it was wrong to blame 20th-century Jews for what some may have done in the first century. That was a big step forward.

Do We Just Talk about Jews or Do We Converse with Jews?

Christian churches had been discussing "the Jewish question" for years. Bonhoeffer had written about it. In the first months of Hitler's coming to power, Bonhoeffer had noted that "the Church is much concerned with the Jewish Question." He suggested people read their Bibles more carefully. Bonhoeffer should also have said, "Talk with your sisters and brothers who are your Jewish neighbours." No one said that then. A Jewish commentator, Michael Wyschogrod,

criticized Vatican statements for being so imper-
sonal, saying, "The non-Christian religions are
spoken *about*, not spoken *to*."

Wyschogrod is a good example of a Jew the
WCC did not simply talk about, but talked to and
worked with. He took part, for example, in the
Faith and Order study *The Roots of Our Common
Faith* in 1983, and was the first Jew to be included
in the Commission on Faith and Order – the
council's body that studies the theological basis for, and challenges to,
church unity. In another study he offered *A Jewish Perspective on Karl
Barth*, his favourite Christian theologian. An even more impressive
example is the case of Gerhart Riegner, Secretary General of the World
Jewish Congress, who was working in Geneva, doing his best to rescue
Jews from Hitler's cruel claws. He needed all the support he could
get, and found in the World Council, which was in formation, much
more help than the International Red Cross, also based in Geneva.
Riegner and Visser 't Hooft wrote joint letters and memoranda to the
British and US governments and to William Temple, Archbishop of
Canterbury – "a unique case," says Riegner, "in the history of Jewish
Christian relations." He adds, "I believe that today the World Council
of Churches is proud to have taken up the defence of the Jews during
those difficult times."[10] Temple, who had been active in the ecumenical movement since serving as a young steward at Edinburgh 1910,
was frustrated that British and US governments took months to reply
to his letters, for with every day's delay, another 10,000 Jews were murdered in Auschwitz.

> **"I believe that today
> the World Council
> of Churches is proud
> to have taken up
> the defence of the
> Jews during those
> difficult times."**

Mission or Ecumenism?

The relationship between church and synagogue was, according to
Karl Barth, *the* ecumenical issue. He wrote in his 1959 book *Church*

Dogmatics: "Even the modern ecumenical movement suffers more seriously from the absence of Israel than of Rome or Moscow."[11]

In preparation for one of the first serious engagements with Roman Catholic scholars, the fourth Faith and Order conference at Montreal in July 1963, the Faith and Order department prepared a paper on "Christ and the Church." In a detailed footnote, they admit that many questions still had to be answered: "It is greatly to be desired that a group be appointed to study the complex and highly debatable questions bound up with the Church's relation to Israel: e.g., the relation of Israel as the covenant people of God to the Church of the New Covenant, considered both historically and theologically; the role of Israel as a nation in the time of the Church."[12] Some of these questions were taken up later. But even in 1963, Faith and Order would have been helped if in their thinking about the church, they followed the pattern being adopted at Vatican II to select as their key New Testament image the church as people of God rather than body of Christ. "Body of Christ" is so obviously a Christian image. "People of God" recalls God's covenant with Israel: "I will be your God, you shall be my people" (Ex.6:7; Deut. 4:20).

Faith and Order expert Paul Minear had already pointed out in 1960 that the New Testament employs nearly a hundred different images in attempts to describe the church. No one image, treated in isolation, is sufficient.[13] It is easier to isolate the church from her Jewish roots if you think of the church as, for example, the bride of Christ, rather than as servant of the Lord, or a royal priesthood. Any annotated edition of the New Testament will give you the essential Old Testament references and background that were employed by New Testament writers to describe the new community of those following Jesus. This is especially true of "people of God," where 1 Peter 2:9–10 clearly relates to Exodus 19:6.

Jesus Was a Jew

Hitler denied this; Barth affirmed this. Jesus is a Jew. Barth preached this in Bonn in 1933, only months after Hitler came to power. Some in the congregation walked out. Luther, in an early writing, had said that Jesus Christ was born a Jew. In earlier times, if Jews converted, they were free from persecution by Christians, but in Hitler's Germany there was no such respite. Once a Jew, always a Jew. Anyone with a Jewish parent was penalized, even if no longer practising the Jewish faith. When the Jewish and Christian scholar Geza Vermes wrote about Jesus the Jew in 1973, he shocked conservative Christians. In 1988, the WCC's anthology of statements, *The Theology of the Churches and the Jewish People*, commented that the Jewishness of Jesus was still "a point of debate." But today, "the Jewishness of Jesus is axiomatic," Vermes said in 2010.[14]

The Hope of Israel and the State of Israel

The distinguished group of top rank theologians who prepared the "Statement of the Hope of Israel" for the Evanston assembly theme hoped that the two subjects would not be confused. They were.[15] The assembly did not adopt this statement and decided "to omit any reference to the hope of Israel in its Statement on the main theme."[16] At the time, it seemed too political for most, and the assembly was not prepared to give the impression that the WCC was endorsing the establishment of the State of Israel. The Vatican would not do so until 1990. In fairness to the minority view, the official Evanston report includes the "Statement on the Hope of Israel" as an appendix. It also lists the 24 delegates who supported it, and a very distinguished group they were: Martin Niemöller, Joseph Hromadka, Marc Boegner, Tom Torrance, Pierre Maury, and Oliver Tomkins, among others. Karl Barth had also signed this statement, but was not present at Evanston. Those who signed wished to make it clear that "our concern in this issue is wholly biblical and is not to be confused with any political attitude toward the State of Israel." What they wished to emphasize was this: "Our hope in Christ's coming victory includes our hope for Israel in Christ, in His victory over the blindness of His own people. To expect Jesus Christ means to hope for the conversion of the Jewish people, and to love Him means to love the people of God's promise." In retrospect, and in the light of the later reflections on Christian–Jewish relationships that I have surveyed, the statement might now seem inadequate. Its positive point remains: thinking about Israel's hopes and Christ, the Messiah of Israel, cannot be separated.

Since Evanston, much has happened in the Middle East to challenge all our best hopes. As I write, the whole region is in turmoil, and much of it due in part to the State of Israel's uneasy relationship with her Arab and Muslim neighbours. But let me conclude this section with a sign of hope. The Porto Alegre assembly welcomed as a Jewish guest Deborah Wiseman. She was delighted to be invited. She had attended many WCC functions over the past 18 years, but this assembly was, she said, "the largest, most diverse and most exciting. What a thrill and a privilege to be living in a time when people of many different traditions can work together as partners in the quest for peace, justice, human rights, an end to racism and oppression. I am grateful to the WCC for giving me this opportunity to be part of your deliberations." She went on to recall how this kind of inter-faith cooperation was foreshadowed in the Hebrew scriptures in the stories of Jethro, the Midianite priest who was father-in-law to Moses, and the accounts of the life-saving deeds of the midwives and the Egyptian Pharaoh's daughter who rescued the infant Moses.[17]

The Ecumenical Accompaniment Programme of the WCC

What has become distinctive in the WCC's response to the way Israel refuses to keep within its 1967 boundaries but constantly encroaches on lands acquired by conquest or outright theft, as in the building of the wall through Palestinian lands, is the Ecumenical Accompaniment Programme. Christian and other volunteers at the checkpoints are there to ease tensions and show solidarity

The State of Israel

The establishment of the State of Israel in 1948 was a major reason why delegates at Evanston were not happy about including a section on "the Hope of Israel" in a paper on the assembly theme. Israel was not just a theological issue, but a political problem, as became even more obvious later. In 2005, Peter Weiderud, as director of the WCC's commission of the Churches on International Affairs, could state that the WCC had devoted more attention to the Arab–Israeli conflict than to any other issue. It did so not only out of Christian concern for human rights, justice, and peace, but also in response to requests from member churches in the Middle East, including the Middle East Council of Churches, established in 1974 and joined in 1990 by the seven Roman Catholic churches of the region.

with the victims and mediate with the victors. The programme was established soon after the Harare Assembly in 1998 by the central committee meeting in Potsdam, Germany, in 2001. But this is not a programme imposed by a distant body. Local churches invited volunteers to come to Israel and Palestine and help them. A seminar in 2005 collected some of their stories. Here is just one.

Vivienne Jackson tells us she is not a religious believer, but she wanted to do something about injustice in Israel/Palestine. She admired the Quakers and their commitment to nonviolence and interfaith work. Through the programme she came to meet Palestinian Muslims and Palestinian Christians, and together they discovered and reinforced each other's beliefs in a common humanity. Did her engagement make a difference to the lives of people she worked with? Certainly! Not least important was the fact that she was Jewish, and so countered the bad impression many Palestinians had of the Jews.

Laos, People of God: Laity

Evanston also rediscovered the laity. Not that lay people were invisible, even in the genesis and formation of the WCC. Lay leaders included John R. Mott, who chaired the International Missionary conference at Edinburgh in 1910 and was present as a consultant at Evanston; Joe Oldham, executive secretary at Edinburgh 1910, then of the International Missionary Council, chief organizer of the Life and Work conference in Oxford in 1937, and honorary president of the WCC at Amsterdam in 1948; and Hendrik Kraemer, the first director of the Ecumenical Institute at Bossey, and author of one of the pioneering studies about the laity. Among women, one could mention Kathleen Bliss, a main speaker at Amsterdam, chair of the committee on the laity and editor of a major study, *The Service and Status of Women in the Churches*; Sarah Chakko, from the Oriental

Orthodox tradition, the first woman to become
a president of the WCC, and the first chair of
the commission of the Life and Work of Women
in the Church; Madeleine Barot, active in the
resistance in France and later director of the
department of the Cooperation of Women and
Men in Church and Society; Pauline Webb, also
a president; and Susan de Diétrich, lay leader in
ecumenical youth and student movements, and long remembered
for her Bible studies. As one of her associates commented: "No one
who heard her expound the Bible will ever forget her incisive mind,
her simplicity of expression and her sense of humour, nor doubt that
the Bible is the living word of God for everyone, as it was for her."[18]

> Sarah Chakko,
> from the Oriental
> Orthodox tradition,
> the first woman to
> become a president
> of the WCC . . .

One might even get the impression that the ecumenical movement was a lay persons' movement and certainly not just of lay men
– though, despite the famous women I have mentioned, it would
be some time before each assembly or central committee aspired to
a more even distribution of places among women and men. And
the brief profiles I have offered make it abundantly obvious that
whatever else "lay" might mean, it does not mean amateur. All such
people were respected experts in their fields. Most of the men – and
the women, if their churches gave them the choice – had come
to the conclusion that one could serve God and his churches just
as well without being ordained and inducted into a pastorate or
becoming part of a hierarchy of presidents and bishops. When the
WCC started to talk about the laity, it could let such lay people do
the talking from their own insights and experience. It was Kraemer
who offered the first major Protestant study of
The Theology of the Laity in 1958, a year before
Yves Congar's *Lay People in the Church*, which
first appeared in French the following year. It
was Kraemer, too, who saw Bossey's role as ini-

> . . . whatever else "lay"
> might mean, it does
> not mean amateur.

tially a centre of lay training, a role that is less evident today, unless one notes the wide range of organizations that benefit from its wonderful location and rich resources. And in this connection, how can one fail to mention Reinold von Thadden-Trieglaff, founder of the German Kirchentag gatherings that began in 1949 with 40,000 people attending and today can muster nearly a million for serious Christian-based discussions on war and peace and other vital issues of the day. Most of those attending are lay and Christian, and not necessarily regular churchgoers, Sunday by Sunday.[19]

The Evanston assembly commended its report, "The Laity: The Christian in His Vocation," to the churches for study and appropriate action, and the churches were asked to report the results of their study and action to the central committee, which would then be meeting before the next assembly, later agreed to be held in New Delhi in 1961. The previous assembly at Amsterdam had declared: "Only by the witness of spiritually intelligent and active laity can the church meet the modern world in its actual perplexities and life situations. Since one of the hard facts of the present time is that millions of people think of the church as floating above the modern world and entirely out of touch with it, the importance of this simple pronouncement cannot easily be overestimated."[20] The report then noted the different ways and the different countries in which the laity were being rediscovered, including lay academies and the German Kirchentag. Von Thadden himself had been present at the Amsterdam assembly and had become active in the WCC. He spoke about the Kirchentag in the debate on this report. As well as commending the report to the churches, the assembly agreed to establish a Department of the Laity. The department in turn published a bulletin, *Laity*. In this bulletin we find examples of numerous experiments and reflections on the theme. Among the most interesting are informed comments on what Roman Catholic bishops at Vatican II agreed about the "Lay Apostolate."

Sixty years after Evanston, we may ask whether the World Council ought still to have such a department, for it ceased to do so in 1971. Basic projects often continue under different titles, and in the case of the laity one can argue that instead of treating "the laity" as a separate issue, lay people themselves were considered in relation to various projects like Justice, Peace and Care for Creation, Being an Inclusive Community, Overcoming Violence, International Affairs, Congregational Life, and the earlier theme adopted at Amsterdam of the "Responsible Society."

In 1993, the WCC held a consultation subtitled *An Exploration of the Role of the Laity in the Church Today*, and published the findings with the main title *A Letter of Christ to the World*. The title recalls what Paul said about the people of God being living letters, and what the New Delhi assembly had said in 1961: that "the real letter written to the world today does not consist of words. We Christian people, wherever we are, are a letter from Christ to the world."[21] The WCC's main journal, *The Ecumenical Review*, devoted a whole issue to "Re-Opening the Ecumenical Discussion of the Laity" in October 1993, and the following year, the central committee meeting in Johannesburg devoted a plenary session to the *Laos Theou*, the people of God. The whole project shows the WCC at its best: wide consultations among member churches in all continents and serious theological reflection from staff members like Hans-Ruedi Weber, who had been active in the Laity Department and at Bossey from the early years and, like several others in the WCC, is also renowned for his Bible studies.

There was no suggestion that the department of the Laity should be re-established, but there was a clear consensus that lay people were frequently forgotten. This is true. It has often been noted that though the concept "people of God" takes precedence in the WCC's most widely studied report, *Baptism, Eucharist and Ministry* (1982), lay people are quietly forgotten after the first six paragraphs, while all attention is then given to bishops, priests, and deacons in the 49 paragraphs that follow. Old habits of thinking of the church as the clergy die hard. But thankfully, real progress is evident in a more recent Faith and Order text, the sequel to *Baptism, Eucharist and Ministry – The Church: Towards a Common Vision* (2013), where descriptions of the church as the people of God, the community of the baptized, the royal priesthood, and so on are more consistently carried through.

The Roman Catholic Church and Laity

Since Vatican II, Roman Catholics, though resisting full membership, have been fully involved in the work of the WCC, particularly in the Faith and Order Commission, which produced the two documents I have just mentioned, and in the Joint Working Group between the WCC and the Roman Catholic Church. Not surprisingly, but as a matter for profound thankfulness, ideas on key concerns like the laity often converge. The Vatican Council made the people of God its key biblical concept and gave it, or should we say gave all of us, priority over considerations of the hierarchy, by which the church had tended to be defined. It also, as noted, produced a whole document on the lay apostolate. But as with the WCC, after the euphoria of the 1960s there was little fresh thinking about lay people in the church and their mission in society. Roman Catholic lay theologian Paul Lakeland is determined to revive the earlier concerns. Churches need to treat their people as mature adults and help them to be such. They can do this partly by enabling them to take a full part in the decision-making processes of the church. Such views are spelled out in more detail in *The Liberation of the Laity* (2003) and at a more popular and even dramatic level in *Catholicism at the Crossroads: How the Laity Can Save the Church* (2007).

All our best theological convictions have biblical roots. The Christians in Corinth were, according to Paul, only "infants in Christ." He had to feed them with milk, not solid food (1 Cor. 3:1-2). Ephesians declares that the task of teachers and preachers is "to equip God's people for work in his service" (Eph. 4:11) and that only together can we reach that maturity which is nothing less than the full stature of Christ. Here then it is also the case that one church may help another, provided that all of us, as in the ideal of "receptive ecumenism," are also ready to learn.

Acting Together

The WCC's activities are no substitute for what the member churches can do and should do together. Hence it was that an important point made at Evanston 1954 had been agreed earlier at the Faith and Order conference at Lund in 1952. The Faith and Order report to the assembly asked the churches "whether they should not act together in all matters except those in which deep differences of conviction compel them to act separately." Sixty years later, this remains an enormous challenge, not least among local congregations where so-called non-theological factors become deeply held convictions.[22]

Even before Evanston, far-sighted but critical ecumenists like Karl Barth had sensed that the council must reach out beyond its European and North American borders. No location was more obvious than the one and only country that had brought episcopal and non-episcopal churches together into a United Church – India, home of the United Church of South India (1947), and later of another pioneering venture, the United Church of North India (1970). So it was to New Delhi that more ecumenical pilgrims journeyed in 1961.

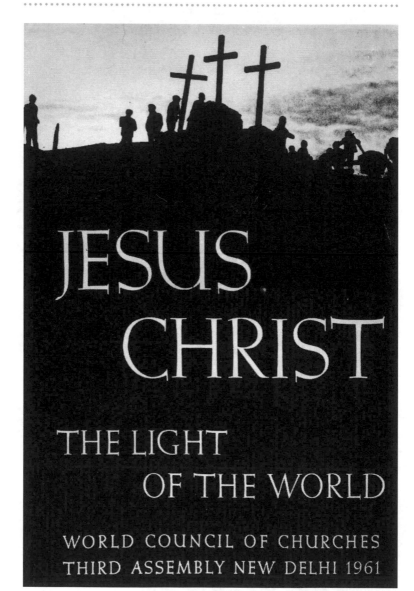

JESUS CHRIST

THE LIGHT
OF THE WORLD

WORLD COUNCIL OF CHURCHES
THIRD ASSEMBLY NEW DELHI 1961

CHAPTER THREE

NEW DELHI 1961
"Jesus Christ, the Light of the World"

Sometimes a different location makes no difference to the conversation. When working with students at Bossey, I once drove some English colleagues round Lake Geneva and was appalled that all they wanted to talk about was Methodist Circuits! Meeting in New Delhi was bound to make a difference. It did.

Mission and Unity: Dialogue with other Living Faiths

The assembly in New Delhi, like the World Mission Conference in Edinburgh (1910), is a landmark in the development of the ecumenical movement and the World Council of Churches (WCC) for several reasons: 1) its unity statement on "all in each place"; 2) being the first assembly held in a country where Christians are only a tiny minority; 3) the integration of the International Missionary Council and the WCC; and 4) most of the Eastern Orthodox churches, particularly those from Eastern Europe, becoming members of the

WCC. This included the Russian Orthodox Church, making it the member church with the largest number of faithful.

The first three developments are closely related and to a large extent are personified in Lesslie Newbigin, the Scottish Presbyterian missionary to India who became one of the first bishops in the pioneering united church, the Church of South India, formed as the country became independent in 1947. It was he who drafted what has remained the best-known unity statement, the first in a long line of descriptions of the unity we seek which would be developed at almost every subsequent assembly. I quote it here and comment on it and the other New Delhi themes later.

> We believe that the unity which is both God's will and his gift to his Church is being made visible as all in each place who are baptized into Jesus Christ and confess him as Lord and Saviour are brought by the Holy Spirit into one fully committed fellowship, breaking the one bread, joining in common prayer, and having a corporate life reaching out in witness and service to all and who at the same time are united with the whole Christian fellowship in all places and all ages in such wise that ministry and members are accepted by all, and that can act and speak together as occasion requires for the tasks for which God calls his people.[1]

The decision of the majority of the Eastern Orthodox churches to become WCC members was a landmark for many Orthodox and non-Orthodox. This is one of the council's achievements since it built bridges between the "first" and the "second" world, just as the massive entrance of churches from the South (also strongly related to New Delhi) was a bridge between the "first" and the "third" world, to use the terminology of that period.

As important as the theme of unity is to the WCC, it is the question of mission that is most associated with the assembly in New Delhi.

A Few Words about Earlier Discussions of "Mission"

Looking back on great events, we often notice things contemporaries didn't see. Sometimes this is because we are only imagining a past that never happened. The World Missionary Conference that met in Edinburgh, Scotland, in 1910 is today heralded as the parent of the founding assembly of the World Council of Churches in Amsterdam 1948 and subsequent assemblies of the WCC, but the actual delegates to the Edinburgh conference had a more restricted agenda. They met to compare missionary methods and learn from each other. As such, Edinburgh belongs to a sequence of world conferences on mission and evangelism which would continue to be held every ten years or so, even after the International Missionary Council became part of the WCC at New Delhi in 1961. It was also a precursor of the Evangelical Congress of Lausanne in 1974. Although Edinburgh 1910 was first advertised as "The Third Ecumenical Missionary Conference," it was never going to qualify as ecumenical since it was limited to representatives of Protestant and Anglican missions. Its delegates seemed blissfully unconcerned that half the Christian world was Roman Catholic but was not invited. And even when the name of the event was changed to World Missionary Conference, its "world" was smaller than ours. Mission was about evangelizing "non-Christian fields," and therefore conference organizers deliberately excluded what we sometimes call "the Christian world" or "Christendom": Europe, North America, Central and South America, the Pacific, the Caribbean, and countries where the majority of the faithful belong to Eastern and Oriental Orthodox churches. Most of the 1,215 delegates were white men, and just a few women, who were

> Most of the 1,215 delegates were white men, and just a few women, who were missionaries from Europe or North America.

missionaries from Europe or North America. Delegates like Wardlaw Thompson of the London Missionary Society took the view that the so-called younger churches were not yet ready to take their place in such exalted company. "Younger"? At least one of these churches, the Mar Thoma Church in India, was much older than the churches most delegates belonged to, having been founded, so it is claimed, by Thomas, one of Jesus' first disciples!

Edinburgh 1910 was celebrated with a centenary conference in that city in 2010 to consider its real legacy.[2] We can now see that it wrestled with a number of challenges that today's World Council of Churches still has to work through – questions such as these:

Can Christians engage in mission without troubling too much about church unity?

Many but not all the European and North American churchmen who set the agenda thought you could. Native leaders from countries like India, China, and Japan thought you could not. The price of gaining the support of bishops like Charles Gore, one of England's leading Anglo-Catholic theologians, was to agree that "no resolution shall be allowed which involves questions of doctrine or church polity" on which churches and societies taking part differ among themselves. But when Cheng Jingyi, a prominent Chinese Protestant church leader, appealed for a United Protestant Church in China, his appeal, said Temple Gairdner, author of the first official report on the conference, only showed how "completely unaware of the real difficulties of uniting Chinese Christians" people like Cheng were.[3] Not so. In 1927, a united Church of Christ in China was formed out of 16 denominational groups. As for India, Brian Stanley, who is now the expert on Edinburgh 1910 and my chief guide in this section, can claim, "The road that led eventually to the formation of the Church of South India in 1947

and the Church of North India in 1970 began in Edinburgh."[4] The
Church of South India is rightly heralded as a breakthrough, in that
for the first time episcopal and non-episcopal churches were united
together as one church. An earlier union, The United Church of
Canada (1925), brought together only Congregationalists, Methodists, and some Presbyterians, whereas the Church of South India
also included Anglicans. The Japanese Federation of Churches,
formed in 1911, is also a legacy of Edinburgh 1910.

What about the churches' role in mission?

Edinburgh accepted that mission was something best left to missionary societies. Leading theologians like Emil Brunner and Karl
Barth would later challenge this. They made the point that the
church is missionary or it is not church. Brunner is still quoted for
saying, "the church exists by mission as fire by burning." Yet the
point about mission remained to be grappled with within the Faith
and Order studies of the church. The first study (1998) spoke of
The Nature and Purpose of the Church. The second, in 2005, put more
emphasis on mission under the title *The Nature and Mission of the
Church*. The opening chapter of the resulting "convergence document," *The Church: Towards a Common Vision* (2012) has the title
"God's Mission and the Unity of the Church." It reflects in that
title much of the pioneer thinking expounded by the South African
theologian David Bosch in his classic survey, *Transforming Mission*.[5]
Missio Dei. Mission is God's, not ours.

And what about inter-faith relations in "mission fields"?

Edinburgh had a commission on "The Christian Message in Relation to Non-Christian Religions." Few then doubted that the Christian faith would triumph. For example, Hindus might come to see
Christ as the fulfiller of their hopes. However, the case of Islam

... **the Spirit of God might be at work in all religions.**

was recognized as more of a challenge. Alfred Garvie, a British Congregationalist, was pessimistic. "Islam is not only later in point of time, but it has borrowed from Christianity as well as from Judaism, degrading what it has borrowed, and it claims the right in virtue of its superiority to supersede and supplant Christianity." Again, in retrospect we might admit that if Islam did claim to supersede Christianity, Christians in turn often claimed that their faith superseded Judaism. John Cairns, the Scottish Presbyterian, commended a more positive and potentially fruitful line when he dared to suggest that the Spirit of God might be at work in all religions.

Delegates to the Edinburgh conference were not yet in the era of inter-faith dialogue and serious listening to each other. The word had yet to be invented. Dialogue became a key word at Vatican II (1962–1965) and at the Commission of World Mission and Evangelism in Mexico in 1963. The veteran ecumenist Norman Goodall, a secretary of the International Missionary Council and assistant secretary of the WCC, comments rather ruefully, "The tendency, not least in the World Council, to fasten on a particular word for a particular occasion and then work it to death has affected the word 'dialogue', but before it is superseded by another verbal fashion its importance should not be overlooked."[6] "Dialogue" will be studied later when we come to the integration of the International Missionary Council and the WCC, which Goodall himself did much to bring about in 1961.

What is the difference between "mission" and "evangelism"? Which has priority?

"Mission and Evangelism" poses another set of questions churches must wrestle with: What is the difference between "mission" and "evangelism"? Which has priority?

And finally, if the immediate sequel to Edinburgh 1910 was the First World War, churches can never evade the question of the link between evangelism and social and political responsibility. How could Christian people shoot and bomb each other?

How Does the WCC Respond to These Challenges?

Delegates to the WCC assembly in New Delhi were aware that unlike a Protestant missionary conference, the WCC could not focus on mission and ignore the issue of unity or the plight of the poor. Those concerned with social and political issues (otherwise known as Life and Work) were meeting in New Delhi as one body with members of the Commission on Faith and Order and with those involved in the work of Mission and Evangelism. There was always the fear that one or other concern would lose out and be marginalized. At the Faith and Order Conference in Edinburgh in 1937, Arthur Headlam, Bishop of Gloucester, opposed the formation of the WCC on the grounds that social and political concerns would now take priority. Perhaps they needed to, as people like Headlam were unable to see the harsh realities of Hitler's tyranny. Another Anglican, John Stott, felt that even before the amalgamation of the International Missionary Council and the WCC, too little had been said about evangelism at Amsterdam 1948, and still not enough at the mission conference in Melbourne in 1980.

Evangelical and Ecumenical

As far as I know, John Stott never met the evangelist John R. Mott (1865–1955). "If any one individual could be said to personify the modern ecumenical movement . . . it would be John R. Mott. In him converge the varied strands of which the ecumenical movement is woven."[7] So wrote Oliver Tomkins (1908–1992), Anglican bishop of Bristol and one-time associate general secretary of the

WCC, in the *Dictionary of the Ecumenical Movement*. Mott, a US Methodist, and Stott, very much the English Evangelical Anglican, were agreed that one could be, and indeed must be, Evangelical and ecumenical. Mott believed in world evangelization, and he pursued this vocation through missions to students and serving as chairman of the International Missionary Conference at Edinburgh 1910. But he also took an active part in the Faith and Order conferences at Lausanne (1927) and Edinburgh (1937), preached at the first assembly of the WCC at Amsterdam (1948), and was a consultant at Evanston, Illinois, in 1954, the year before he died. John Stott, at an international gathering of Evangelical missiologists convened by the WCC at Stuttgart in 1987, said the distinction between Evangelical and ecumenical Christians was "a misleading classification since an increasing number of us belong to the overlap" of the two.[8] Would that it were so. But he would have applauded what John Mott said in 1925: "The unity or oneness among His followers down the generations, for which Christ prayed, was not to be regarded as an end in itself but rather as a means to ensure the great central end of Christian missions, namely that "the world may believe" (John 17:21). Cecil Roebeck Jr, speaking for the Pentecostals on the Centenary of Edinburgh 1910, said, "This admonition bears repeating in 2010."

Mission and Evangelism

Evangelicals like Stott look for certain key expositions of the gospel in any mission statement and are often disappointed at what the WCC says or fails to say. Was enough said about Jesus? Evangelicals at Harare in 1998 were shocked that in the Africa plenary, Jesus did not even get a mention, and that despite the theme text "Turn to God, Rejoice in Hope," there was lacking in the assembly "a strong emphasis on mission, evangelism and the church."[9]

Mission to Six Continents

Much more should be said on this theme, voiced at the Mexico City missionary conference in 1963, than I have space for here. The best person to say it is Lesslie Newbigin. "Mission to Six Continents" is the chapter he wrote in *A History of the Ecumenical Movement, Volume Two, 1948–1968*. It was Newbigin who, with Norman Goodall, helped bring about the integration of the International Missionary Council with the WCC at New Delhi. If everywhere is now a "mission field," local congregations need to be equipped for mission.

At the same time, delegates authorized a study, "The Missionary Structure of the Congregation," in order to equip congregations for mission as the assembly accepted that the church's mission field is everywhere, not just "overseas." The reports presented to the assembly are still worth studying, for they engaged some of the best-known theologians and sociologists: Hans Margull, J.C. Hoekendijk, Walter Hollenweger, Thomas Wieser, Colin Williams, Peter Berger, Werner Simpendörfer, Paul Löffler, and Letty Russell. Its common theme echoes Bonhoeffer: "A truly missionary congregation is a community for others."[10] Thirty years later, when many churches in Europe were searching for new ways to communicate or coping with the sudden collapse of years of communist suppression, the WCC offered many helpful examples of local initiatives in a compendium entitled *Hear What the Spirit Says to the Churches: Towards Missionary Congregations in Europe*.[11]

Writing in the turbulent 1960s, when almost everything was being questioned, Newbigin comments, "During the years in which drastic changes of structure were being made, those involved largely took the content of the gospel for granted. Today that can no longer be done."[12] Missionary societies by their very nature were expected to sing with confidence, "We have a gospel to proclaim."[13] Kirsteem Kim, writing about New Delhi 40 years later as she and others prepared a new statement on mission for Busan, wondered whether greater efforts should have been made to give the missionary societies a stronger place in the WCC, rather than assume too quickly that the churches would fulfil their role.[14]

In *Evangelism in Eclipse: World Mission and the World Council of Churches,* Harvey Hoekstra from North America argues that the decision in New Delhi to integrate a body composed of representatives of missionary societies, the International Missionary Council, and the WCC was never unanimous. Some key people like Stephen Neill, John V. Taylor, and M.A.C. Warren had reservations. He felt

After Busan: Mission in Changing Landscapes

In the current WCC mission statement as presented to the Busan assembly in 2013, we retain some familiar headings but explore them from a different perspective. The new title is *Together towards Life: Mission and Evangelism in Changing Landscapes.* As with all key documents, it is now possible to download the text from the WCC's website. We have taken on board much that had been written by David Bosch and others about God's mission: "The missionary God who sent the Son into the world."[16] As Kirsteen Kim explained in introducing the report to the assembly, "Mission is participation in the work of the life-giving Spirit. . . . 'Evangelism is a confident but humble sharing of our faith and conviction with other people.'"[17] At various points in the document, the contents of our Christian faith are spelled out with a strong emphasis, as in the title, that Christ has come that we may have life, life in all its fullness (John 10:10).

his fears were well founded that in the WCC, evangelism would cease to be a priority, but is honest enough to admit that even before New Delhi, there was less confidence about world evangelization despite the constant reminder that there were still three billion people who had never heard the gospel. For the other side of the argument, one need only read books by Newbigin and Goodall stating that the churches and not just missionary societies must be missionary.[15] "The dilemma with which I constantly wrestled was how to achieve a permeation of all the activities of the council with a missionary concern," wrote Newbigin in his autobiography, *Unfinished Agenda* (1985).

Personal Salvation, Social and Political Responsibility, Holistic Mission

Evangelicals tend to put the emphasis on personal salvation; the WCC tends to emphasize social responsibility. Both groups could be challenged and were being challenged to do both. When Evangelicals met together at Lausanne in 1974, largely thanks to the influence of the US evangelist Billy Graham, it was John Stott who convinced the congress to agree to a covenant that also included social and political responsibility. Clause 4 is all about evangelism. Clause 5 is about Christian social responsibility. No attempt was made to relate the one to the other or to state which had precedence, partly because the followers of Graham and the followers of Stott could not agree. Stott himself noted this point in his comments on the sequel to Lausanne in a volume he edited, *Making Christ Known: Historic Mission Documents from the Lausanne Movement, 1974–1989.* Later, in 1982, at a meeting at Grand Rapids, Michigan, Evangelical leaders would address the issue.

Stott, like a good evangelist, was responding to the word of God in the Bible, but was aware that we may often see only what we are looking for. Our vision can be distorted by our own culture. As he became a global traveller and met Christians from Latin America, Africa, and Asia, lands where most people experienced chronic poverty, he came to see that the Great Commission, "Go therefore to all nations and make them my disciples . . . and teach them to observe all that I have commanded you" (Matt. 28:19–20) must be related to other texts, such as Luke 4, on "good news for the poor" and "release for prisoners." Our understanding of mission and evangelism needed to be more holistic. This was also the conclusion reached 12 years later in the WCC's mission statement *Together towards Life: Mission and Evangelism in Changing Landscapes,* adopted at Busan. Maybe Stott had helped pioneer the way. By "holistic," Busan meant also embracing creation. Stott, a great lover of God's creation, would not disagree.

Stott recognized that the desire of Evangelicals the world over to hold their own congress in 1974 "must unfortunately be understood, at least in part, as a loss of confidence in the World Council of Churches." He added, "the leaders of the World Council have also been justly critical of many of us evangelicals for our lack of social concern."[18] His biographer notes that at Uppsala 1968, Stott welcomed the wide range of concerns that the assembly had for race relations, refugees, world development, hunger, and war, but regretted that there seemed to be "no comparable compassion for the spiritual hunger of the unevangelized millions, no comparable call to them with the Bread of Life." Stott believed that Jesus Christ was saying to the WCC what he once said to the Pharisees about their concern for ceremonial observances: "These you ought to have done, without neglecting the others."[19] Twelve years later, two approaches remained polarized. At the WCC's World Mission and Evangelism Conference at Melbourne in May 1980, the cries of the poor, hungry, and oppressed predominated. At the Evangelical meeting at Pattaya, Thailand, a month later, one heard more about hunger and thirst for the gospel.[20] Some delegates were present at both. Did they acquire a more holistic understanding?

Mission and Dialogue

Bishop Michael Nazir-Ali was born in Pakistan to Christian and Muslim parents. At first a Muslim, he became a Christian at the age of 15, and was later the Anglican bishop of Rochester, England. While his background might or might not make him the ideal participant in dialogue, he certainly is well placed to write a book entitled *Mission and Dialogue*. The subtitle shows his personal bias to mission: *Proclaiming the Gospel Afresh in Every Age*. He criticizes the WCC for being too ambivalent, and WCC's 1989 world mission conference at San Antonio, Texas, for arguing that the occasion of dialogue must not be an occasion for Christian witness.[21]

Nazir-Ali was not at San Antonio. Neither was I. Having read the conference report,[22] I think his criticism is unfair. He fails to appreciate that ecumenical thinking about mission and dialogue has matured slowly since Edinburgh 1910, and has done so more recently because of face-to-face encounters with peoples of other living faiths in the very places that Edinburgh 1910 prioritized – non-Christian lands, like India or Pakistan. When John R. Mott wrote *The Moslem World Today*, he was describing a world in 1925 that we no longer recognize. Then it seemed obvious to this great evangelist that Islam was disintegrating. Only Christ and his programme could fill the vacuum caused by its collapse. Though Mott urged a sympathetic approach to Muslims, he argued that we must aim to present "the message of the living Christ and his redemptive Gospel."[23] A similar assumption prevailed in 1938, when the Dutch Reformed theologian Hendrik Kraemer (1888–1965) was commissioned by the International Missionary Council to write the preparatory volume for the Tambaram missionary conference in India, which he did under the title *The Christian Message in a Non-Christian World*.[24] Christianity was of a totally different order from other religions. Although he had studied Islam and worked in Indonesia from 1922 to 1937, those with even deeper experience of living with peoples of other faiths criticized his views as far too exclusive. Was it really the case that Hindus or Muslims had no experience of God? Kraemer might claim that he was only reflecting what he called "biblical realism" and the theology of Karl Barth, but on both points he might be challenged, not least by Barth, whose own views on other faiths were gently modified as he progressed with the writing of his *Church Dogmatics*.[25]

By the time we come to San Antonio in 1989, missionary thinking, at least in WCC circles, is reaching a more balanced consensus, summed up in this sentence: "We cannot point to any other way of salvation than Jesus Christ, at the same time we cannot set limits to the saving power of God."[26] This is very similar to the claims sometimes made by the Orthodox Church in diaspora: "We know where the true Church is. We do not know where it is not." In this way it is perfectly possible to make a strong, positive affirmation of one's faith while recognizing that we are not in a position to be categorical about other people's beliefs.

Perhaps speaking of consensus about not being able to set limits to God's saving power is claiming too much. The Roman Catholic theologian Bradford Hinze commends the World Council of Churches for giving a strong lead in experiments in inter-religious dialogue but thinks the issue remains "openly contentious" within the WCC.[27] He reminds us what happened at the Canberra assembly in 1991 when Korean theologian Chung Hyuan Kyung invoked the spirits of Hagar, Tiananmen Square, Earth, Air, Water, and our brother Jesus, claiming that without listening to these spirits, we cannot hear the voice of the Holy Spirit. For some, this was inspiration; for others, syncretism. In response to an Orthodox critic,

Kyung replied, "We have been listening to your intellectualisms for 2000 years . . . please listen to us."[28] Rather than claim consensus, it is more helpful to cite various commentators.

Andrew Wingate reminds us that "interfaith dialogue has been a necessity of life for Indian Christians long before it was defined by this technical phrase."[29] Soon after his ordination as an Anglican priest, he taught at Tamil Nadu, and in more recent years has guided discussions at Bossey, where students from three religious traditions, Christianity, Judaism, and Islam, meet and worship together for a month. His experience of working in multi-faith cities like Birmingham and Leicester makes him something of an expert on dialogue. So we take heed when, for example, he tells us that minority religious groups like Jews in England will enter into dialogue only if they are confident that Christians are not just out to convert them.

Stanley Samartha, the first director of the WCC's sub-unit on Relations with Peoples of Other Living Faiths, formed in 1971, says that one lesson that has been learned is that dialogue should deal with specific common human concerns in the community. He adds this summary: "What we need today is a theology that is not less but more true to God by being generous and open, a theology not less but more loving towards the neighbour by being friendly and willing to listen, a theology that does not separate us from fellow human beings but supports us in our common struggles and hopes."[30]

Roman Catholics now speak of "a dialogue of life."[31] Samartha would add, "The church is not [only] called to supply means of livelihood to people but to provide reasons for living."[32] I have added the word "only." I am sure Samartha, living in a land, India, where millions still starve, would agree.

> "What we need today is a theology that . . . does not separate us from fellow human beings but supports us in our common struggles and hopes."

Wesley Ariarajah pleads that "Christians are not the only ones who believe in God's action in the world." Dialogue presumes that God has other witnesses.[33] Ariarajah, a Methodist theologian from Sri Lanka, has also served as a director of the WCC's Inter-Faith Programme. Hans Ucko, a former member of the Inter-Faith Programme staff, stresses that dialogue is not possible without love. These and

Saving the Planet

As noted in an earlier chapter, churches have come to believe that "God so loved the world" does not mean that God only loves me or even all of us human beings. What about the animals? What about the earth? What about this vast universe, whose borders disappear in endless space when we attempt to measure the immeasurable in millions of light years? Here it is sufficient to note that the WCC's new mission statement, adopted at the Busan assembly in 2013, affirms that the gospel is good news for every part of creation and challenges the churches to overcome economic and ecological injustice.[35] In 1991, Newbigin said that neither capitalism nor communism had shown any capacity to care for creation. Both lacked a sense of the transcendent.[36] This was a task for the churches. And though such concern seems new, it should not be. The first book of the Bible contains the story of the flood. The animals, too, are saved, and the covenant is symbolized by a rainbow in the sky. The last book, Revelation, tells of a new heaven and a new earth. Creation is not just the backdrop for the drama of human salvation. It, too, will always be the Creator's saving concern. He alone can make all things new.

other successive WCC inter-faith staff members and directors bring years of living with people of other living faiths to this task. The WCC's programme is no mere academic and abstract exercise.

Dialogue or Damnation?[34]

Listing various comments side by side is irritating if we are looking for WCC decisions. Dialogue is not like that. It encourages us all to join in the conversations, something more of us can easily do as our local communities become multi-faith. The stark alternative to dialogue is damnation. This was the stance taken at the Council of Florence when it condemned to hell all who did not belong to the Catholic Church, and when Christians turned mission into brutal crusades or stood and watched when Jews and their synagogues went up in flames. By contrast, even if we still feel that proclaiming the gospel is our priority, we are bound to act with greater humility and sensitivity. We have sometimes made it hard for other people to believe in Christ.

The next assembly, at Uppsala, would take as its theme text the words of Jesus in Revelation 21:5 – "I am making all things new." But it would do so in a manner that would shock many who had more traditional ideas of what mission and unity were all about. I can say this with some feeling, since the man who wrote the Uppsala report was a member of my congregation here in Oxford – Norman Goodall, a close colleague of Lesslie Newbigin's. I loved him dearly, but we did not always agree!

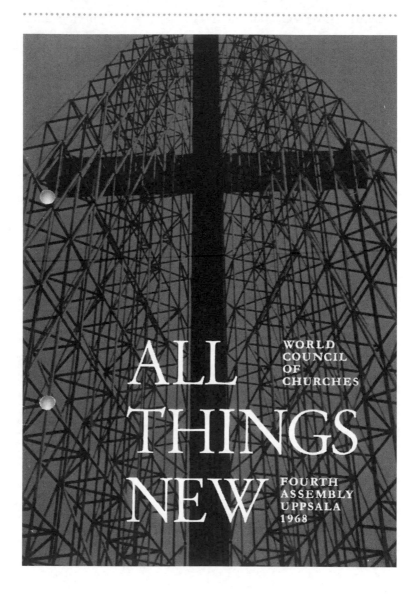

ALL
THINGS
NEW

WORLD
COUNCIL
OF
CHURCHES

FOURTH
ASSEMBLY
UPPSALA
1968

CHAPTER FOUR

UPPSALA 1968
"All Things New"

Weary pilgrims after a long journey may forget how exciting parts of that journey have been. "Bliss was it in that time to be alive, / But to be young was very heaven!" said the poet William Wordsworth. But not all found the 1960s so exciting. Among Roman Catholics, Hans Küng did, whereas his colleague Joseph Ratzinger, the future Pope Benedict XVI, did not. In England, Bishop John Robinson's book *Honest to God* became a bestseller, thanks to newspaper headlines reading, "Bishop says 'God is not a Daddy in the sky'."[1] Did we ever think he was? In the United States, there was much soul searching about the rights and wrongs of the Vietnam War. Uppsala picked up the vibes of such a turbulent decade. The following account outlines some key themes; it is harder, 50 years later, to convey the enthusiasm they generated.

WCC and Rome after Vatican II: Hope for a Genuinely Ecumenical Council

"The world was writing the agenda for this meeting," writes Norman Goodall, the editor of the *Uppsala Report*.[2] It is easy to see why. A lot was happening in 1968: student revolts in many European cities, the so-called Prague Spring in Czechoslovakia, civil war in Nigeria-Biafra, the Vietnam War and controversy about US bombing, the aftermath in the Middle East of the Six-Day War of 1967 and disputes which continue to this day about Israel's occupations of territories taken in that war, and the assassination of the black civil rights leader the Rev. Dr Martin Luther King. Kenneth Slack, a veteran reporter, like Goodall, on World Council of Churches (WCC) events, commented, "what a salutary preventative it was for any superficially optimistic reading of the theme text 'Behold, I make all things new' that the preacher who had been chosen by the churches of the world to expound it had been brutally murdered a matter of weeks before the Assembly met."[3] The 1960s, in retrospect, did seem overly optimistic about human progress. Barth made this same criticism of the Vatican document on the church in the modern world, *Gaudium et Spes* (joy and hope).

One victim of white racism had been silenced, but another well-known black writer, James Baldwin, gave a strong and critical address when the assembly tackled the theme "White Racism or World Community?" Baldwin said, "I address you as one of the creatures, one of God's creatures, whom the Christian Church has most betrayed."[4] Betrayed because he was black, but also because the revivalist group he once belonged to rejected his Jewish friends.[5]

Baldwin described himself as an outsider, though he was the son of a Baptist pastor. Those inside the churches and active inside the ecumenical movement could be just as critical. There was much to criticize. The city of Uppsala, justly famous for producing great Christian leaders like Nathan Söderblom, pioneer of the Life and Work movement in the WCC, and Dag Hammarskjöld, a devout Christian and secretary general of the United Nations, was also located in a country where most take their Christian faith for granted and rarely go to church. Why was this? Had the churches failed? Here was no place for complacency. Youth delegates were highly critical of what they perceived as paternalism and churches being out of touch with the real world. "We did not come here as simple spectators, or to sanction and consent with a passive presence," they said. Ms Adler, a youth delegate from Berlin, warned about temptations facing ecumenism: clericalism, triumphalism, and verbalism.[6] The assembly was acutely aware of "a crisis of worship and behind it a widespread crisis of faith" and the "Challenge of Secularisation."[7] It needed to be reminded, and was reminded, of the danger of succumbing to the very challenges it was so good at describing. Goodall notes the strong hint voiced at Uppsala: "Perhaps, for the sake of the world, the next assembly should be more theological." It is theology, thinking about what God has done and is doing, that gives the church her distinctive voice. Kenneth Slack, great Christian preacher that he was, could not help noticing that "in some 400 words of the youth's declaration there is no reference to God, Jesus, discipleship, worship or religion in any form."

Much of the best theological thinking since the previous assembly, at New Delhi in 1961, had been done at the Second Vatican Council in Rome (1962–1965). The World Council of Churches and large church families represented in its membership were invited to send observers. Some 200 non–Roman Catholic observers had been actively involved in the discussions of key documents on the church, Christian unity, and relations with other faiths. Worship, joy, and hope – or, as they said in Latin,

> Much of the best theological thinking since the previous assembly . . . had been done at the Second Vatican Council in Rome.

gaudium et spes, though it was only the Roman Catholic bishops who could debate and decide. Vatican II was the most geographically universal Christian council ever held, with some 2,500 bishops coming from every continent. It was the most ecumenically generous in its invitations to separated brethren, asking them to please come and help renew the church, the church to which half the world's Christians belong. The council expressed appreciation instead of anathema – the age-old habit, so evident in Trent, of denouncing everyone you disagreed with: "Let him be anathema!" The World Council had helped select a representative group of observers, and most major traditions were glad to respond, though some needed more encouragement than others. Many of the observers not only represented their own confessional bodies, but were also noted experts in the World Council's Faith and Order commission.[8] And though the WCC's general secretary, W.A. Visser 't Hooft, had himself been rather cautious about getting too involved in a Roman Catholic event, when he attended one of its sessions he quickly came to this conclusion: *nostra res agitur,* or "what is going on here in Rome concerns us all." Indeed it did, and still does.

Impact of Vatican II on the Uppsala Assembly

The Second Vatican Council had an immediate impact on the assembly and many of its subsequent activities. Prior to the council, Rome had taken no part in the earlier ecumenical conferences at Edinburgh (1910), Stockholm (1925), Lausanne (1927), and the two held in 1937, one in Oxford the other at Edinburgh, though some ecumenically minded theologians like Congar had shown great interest in these events. From 1928 until shortly before the council, Rome had formally forbidden any Roman Catholic participation. Pope John XXIII's surprise announcement of a council, made during the Week of Prayer for Christian Unity in January

1959, marked a dramatic change even before the council met for the first time in October 1962. Roman Catholics, who had not been allowed to attend the first two WCC assemblies at Amsterdam and Evanston, were now free to attend the assembly that met in New Delhi in 1961. There, Visser 't Hooft welcomed five observers authorized by Pope John's Secretariat for Christian Unity. He quoted his Lutheran colleague Edmund Schlink, who would later be a most active observer at Vatican II: "It would indeed mean much for Christendom and the world, if it became clear . . . that these councils do not meet against each other and that each does not seek its own advantage, but seeks only to serve the Lord Jesus Christ."[9] What was different at Uppsala was that the Roman Catholics were officially appointed delegated representatives and one of them, the Jesuit Roberto Tucci, was invited to address the assembly. Tucci was the editor of a highly respected Jesuit journal, *La Civiltà Cattolica*, and had been active in preparations for the council and later in helping other journalists to report on its proceedings. There are numerous references to his key role in the "official" five-volume *History of Vatican II*.[10]

"We approach your Assembly in a new way, not only with deep and sincere respect but also with a very strong feeling that we are really participating in it,"[11] Tucci said. He spoke highly of the WCC as "the largest and most representative ecumenical organization," and said that for this and many other reasons, it was important for the Roman Catholic Church to engage in "mutual consultation" with the WCC and even contemplate becoming a full member. He accepted that for the time being, this was not being commended – the Joint Working Group between the Roman Catholic Church and the WCC had put this aside for the moment – but the issue could not be evaded. His address is printed in a full in the official report. It reads well, as one might expect from a skilled journalist, but is also the result of careful scholarship and wide reading, as the abundant footnotes in the

A Joint Group on Working Together

The Uppsala Report includes an account of the first meeting of the Joint Working Group between the Roman Catholic Church and the World Council of Churches. This joint body, still very active, was established by the Council and met for the first time at Bossey in December 1965. In its second report, it outlined cooperation already taking place in six areas of collaboration:

1. Faith and worship, including now full Roman Catholic membership in the Faith and Order commission
2. Unity and mission, with collaboration in missionary training and missionary theology
3. Partnership in a major laity congress in Rome in 1967
4. Church and society, development, justice and peace
5. Service activities, including cooperation between Inter-Church Aid and Caritas
6. International affairs, including a joint statement on the conflict in Nigeria

The Joint Working Group agreed with what Fr Tucci had said: "The relations between the Roman Catholic Church and the World Council of Churches need further exploration."

printed text make clear. Tucci had listened to Visser 't Hooft, Eugene Blake, and Lukas Vischer in the WCC; to other Protestant theologians, like Karl Barth and Harvey Cox; and to the Roman Catholic convictions expressed in the documents of Vatican II, speeches by Pope Paul VI, and the theologies of Karl Rahner, Jerome Hamer, Pierre Duprey, and Thomas Stransky, among others. There is nothing in the official statements of Vatican II or the Toronto Declaration of the WCC that prevents the growing involvement of the Church of Rome in the one ecumenical movement. Rome is not the centre: "The centre of the ecumenical movement can only be Christ himself who, through the action of his Spirit, is drawing us all by the way of repentance towards the fullness of unity."[12] To which one hopes the whole assembly voiced a loud "Amen!"

Tucci said he looked forward to the discussion on "The Holy Spirit and the Catholicity of the Church." He had read the preparatory paper and was anxious to know what other churches made of it – not least Rome's sister churches, "the venerable Orthodox Churches," which were now, since New Delhi, so active in the WCC. I love the fact that Tucci clearly relishes ecumenical encounters and says, "We Roman Catholics look forward with *joy* and very special interest to the discussion."[13] He could claim that the choice of theme had been prompted by the honest way Vatican II dealt with catholicity in openly stating that the Roman Catholic Church could not be fully catholic without us. The Decree on Ecumenism, *Unitatis Redintegratio*, admits that "the divisions among Christians prevent the Church from realizing in practice the fullness of catholicity proper to her, in those of her sons and daughters who, though attached to her by baptism, are yet separated from full communion with her."[14]

Tucci was not the only Roman Catholic to be formally invited to address the assembly. He was joined by Lady Jackson (Dr Barbara Ward), a British economist, who addressed the assembly on the theme of rich and poor nations. "In every wealthy country we Christians are a minority large enough, if organized, to make a political impact, to worry legislators, to swing elections . . . to put the world's miseries above the upward drift of our ample domestic comforts," she said.[15] She could have said the same at the Second Vatican Council; many Roman Catholics hoped she would, but being a layperson and a woman, she was prevented from doing so.[16]

The council and a WCC assembly may have common concerns, but they operate in very different ways. The council is a council of bishops. In the assembly, all delegates, men or women, ordained or lay, can ask to speak. But the one type of gathering can sometimes challenge the other to change its ways. In 1971, just three years after Uppsala, Barbara Ward became the first woman to address a synod of Roman Catholic bishops.

Dialogue Takes Time and Demands Patience

Nearly 40 years after the creation of the Joint Working Group between WCC and the Roman Catholic Church, an Anglican delegation to the WCC was rather impatient that no progress had been made on this issue. It is not that simple. This is one of those occasions where one might wish Geneva's critics were better informed. The WCC is made up of national churches. The Roman Catholic Church is an international body. WCC assemblies and committees embrace lay and ordained, women and men. Roman Catholic councils, like Vatican II, are restricted to bishops, all of them men. Half the world's Christians are Roman Catholic; should half of the members of WCC governing bodies be Roman Catholic, too? It is true that thanks to Vatican II's commitment to the restoration of unity with other Christians, Roman Catholics are now active partners in most regional and national councils of churches. It is also true that, despite Vatican II, questions of the authority of councils and collegiality versus the papacy remain unresolved. Tucci cheerfully told the Uppsala assembly that "the Second Vatican Council is the supreme authority of our Church."[17] I am not sure that Pope Paul VI – and later, popes John Paul II and Benedict XVI, would agree. Pope Francis might. For all such weighty reasons, the question of full membership of the Roman Catholic Church is not on the current agenda. What is being explored with Roman Catholics is their full participation in a Global Christian Forum. I shall say more about that in chapter ten.

Of the six areas of joint collaboration, Faith and Order merits special mention. We can now demonstrate great areas of agreement between Roman Catholics, Orthodox, Anglicans, and Protestants on *Baptism, Eucharist and Ministry* (*BEM*, 1982) and currently on "the convergence text": *The Church: Towards a Common Vision* (2013). *BEM*, as it is affectionately known, is especially significant. It was the most widely read Faith and Order document ever produced. Its reception by the member churches was fully reported in detailed documents that currently comprise six volumes plus a summary. There we can read general comments that we now need to pay more attention to ecclesiology and the study of the nature and mission of the church – precisely what we are now doing – and from Roman Catholics that some of us need to think more deeply about sacraments. In both *BEM* and *The Church*, we are all reminded of some of the disagreements, such as the ordination of women, that need to be openly debated. At the Faith and Order conference at Santiago de Compostela (1993), it was also agreed that we need to consider the delicate and obviously personal question of the papacy of the bishop of Rome.[18] John Paul II invited us to do this in his Ecumenical Encyclical *Ut Unum Sint* (1995). Especially remarkable in his appeal were the frequent references to Faith and Order documents and the work of the World Council. Even at Vatican II, neither body was ever mentioned!

Vatican II's document on ecumenism commended dialogues with other churches. Since the council, Roman Catholics have engaged in dialogues with Anglicans, Baptists, Disciples of Christ, Lutherans, Mennonites, Methodists, Reformed, Eastern and Oriental Orthodox churches, Pentecostals, and Evangelicals. These, and the conversations between other confessional groupings, now comprise three hefty volumes published by the WCC as Faith and Order Papers.[19]

We are talking to each other. And listening! Praise the Lord! For nearly 400 years, between the Council of Trent (1545–1563) and Vatican II (1962–1965), we rarely spoke. Ignoring each other only aggravated old divisions and added new ones. The Blessed Virgin Mary was not the subject of Reformation disputes. She has become such since. Today we are learning from each other to respect the Mother of our Lord. The Reformers did not query that as such, Mary was also "Mother of God," *Theotokos*. This had been agreed at Ephesus in 431 before most of the major divisions in the church occurred.[20]

A Genuinely Universal Council

The Uppsala Report, *The Holy Spirit and the Catholicity of the Church*, included this exciting proposal: "The members of the World Council of Churches, committed to each other, should work for the time when a genuinely universal council may once more speak for all Christians, and lead the way into the future."[21] There had just been a universal council, Vatican II, the most geographically universal Christian council ever held. Why not say so? Some at Uppsala had been there and were quite excited by the experience. They had been made to feel they were part of the council. And in the two final sessions there had even been women present – only a few, but then at Edinburgh 1910 and even at Amsterdam 1948 there were fewer than at the council. But spurred on, let us hope, said the Uppsala assembly, that next time we will *all* meet in a council that is *genuinely* universal, and *genuinely* ecumenical: that is, one not confined to Roman Catholic bishops who were, by definition, celibate men.

This far-reaching proposal has behind it a short history going back to Amsterdam 1948, and a longer account that begins with Nicaea 325 or the Jerusalem council described in Acts 15. The short history takes us back to Visser 't Hooft's and the Toronto Declaration's attempts to explain what the WCC is and is not. At Amsterdam the general secretary stated, "We are a Council of Churches, not *the* Council of the one undivided Church. Our name indicates our weakness and our shame before God, for there can be and there *is* only one Church of Christ on earth." He is arguing that if the churches were united, they would be able to meet and make decisions in a genuinely universal council. The Toronto Declaration, *The Church, the Churches and the World Council of Churches* (1950), made it possible for churches which did not recognize each other as churches and might disagree about the nature of the unity we seek to live and work together in such a body as the WCC, provided also that the WCC was seen as only a provisional arrangement or what Visser 't Hooft called "an emergency solution – a stage on the road."[22]

Pope John XXIII made an announcement that created great ecumenical interest in ecumenical councils, an interest that, on and off, flourishes to this day. He spoke of an ecumenical council of the universal church, and it soon became clear that what he had in mind was something more welcoming and inclusive than the Council of Trent or Vatican I, which in Rome's eyes could also be described as ecumenical councils.[23] The meaning of "ecumenical" was one of the points to be clarified, as many of the council fathers had never heard the word being applied to other churches! They would not have read Visser 't Hooft's lecture on the theme "The Meaning of Ecumenical," delivered at Church House, London, in 1953, and later published. But because the WCC had given the word a wider meaning, there was wider interest in councils. Hans Jochen Margull, who later became the WCC's leader for the mission project The Missionary Structure of the Congregation, edited a set of articles by different confessions about how each understood general councils. His study, *Die ökumenischen Konzile der Christenheit*, first appeared in 1961. The book's translation into English exposed another problem. German has different words for councils, so that in German the WCC becomes Ökumenische *Rat der Kirchen* and makes no

Can different and
divided churches make
decisions together,
and if so, how?

claim to be a *Konzil*. In English, we use the same word for the town council as for Vatican II. The two are not the same! At New Delhi (1961), the World Council of Churches, partly in response to the pope's announcement, promoted its own study of the synods and councils of the ancient church. This was published in 1968 as *Councils and the Ecumenical Movement* (in German, *Konzile und die* Ökumenische *Bewegung*).[24]

The question behind such research remains urgent and imperative for today. Can different and divided churches make decisions together, and if so, how? We can turn to the early councils for guidance, because we did so once. Nicaea (325) and Constantinople (381) would be recognized by almost all churches, because they gave us all the creed we still recite today – the commonly called Nicene Creed, more correctly titled the Nicene-Constantinopolitan Creed (381). It is the creed which has the best claim to be ecumenical, in that in its original form it is acceptable to the East and the West, the Anglican Communion, and churches of the Reformation. It is also the key text in the Faith and Order study *Confessing the One Faith*.[25] The Council of Ephesus (431) was accepted by the reformers for what it said about Mary as "Mother of God," *Theotokos*, though Calvin preferred to speak of "Mother of the Son of God." Chalcedon (451) came to stand for what became known as "Chalcedonian Orthodoxy," concerning the two natures of Christ.

But at this stage, major divisions already appear for some of the most ancient churches in the world: Coptic, Syrian, Armenian, Ethiopian, Eritrean, and Malankara churches did not accept Chalcedon. Anglicans and churches of the Reformation accept the first four councils; Eastern Orthodox, the first seven. After that, the matters become more controversial. Who has authority to convene such a council? Roman Catholics would say the pope, but would have to admit that the early councils were convened by the emperor.

Constantine, the first Christian emperor, summoned the bishops to Nicaea partly out of concern to establish peace in the empire. Emperors Gratian and Theodosius summoned bishops to Constantinople to counter the views of the Arians, who were thought to be undermining belief in the divinity of Christ. Ephesus offers an interesting precedent. Nestorius felt his theology had been misunderstood, and so urged emperor Theodosius II to convene a council, which he did. Pope Leo I was at first opposed to the calling of a council at Chalcedon, but since the emperor Marcian wished it, the pope accepted his authority and dutifully sent his legates to share in it. All this information about the emperors' calling of councils one can glean from a good Jesuit historian, Norman Tanner,[26] so let no one accuse me of Protestant bias! But it was the papacy's influence that created problems for the medieval conciliar movement and later for the reformers. Prior to the Reformation, there was an unresolved issue about final authority in the church. Did it reside in the pope, as Vatican I would affirm, or in a council, with its claim to represent the church as a whole? Had that issue been resolved and a reforming council held, the 16th-century Reformation and subsequent divisions might never have happened. Even a council held just before Luther's protest of 1517 failed to carry out much-needed reforms, as it was said, "in head and members." Despite such disappointments, both Luther and Calvin dared to hope that "a free, general Christian Council," one summoned by the emperor and not controlled by the pope, might be able to resolve the issues in dispute. All that happened was Trent, too little and too late.

The good experience of Vatican II which many delegates at Uppsala could vouch for revived such hopes. But general secretary Visser 't Hooft and those who had been present as observers at the council would note that it was still not as free and reforming as the reformers had hoped. The pope and curia controlled the agenda on some subjects. Very big subjects, like the service and status of women in the church, which were being openly discussed in the WCC and its member churches, were off limits at Vatican II. And although for the most part popes John XXIII and Paul VI let the councillors get on with their debates, Paul VI altered some important phrases in the *Decree on Ecumenism*, and despite *Lumen Gentium*'s carefully balanced statements on the Virgin Mary, decided unilaterally to declare that Mary is "Mother of the Church." Why summon 2,500 bishops from all around the world, and spend hours, if not years, reaching consensus, if in the end a pope can declare "this is what we believe"? The observers – and not only the observers, but also ecumenically minded people like Congar – were very troubled at this relapse into the Vatican I style of operating. Uppsala, without actually saying so, dared to hope for something much better than Vatican II, while still rejoicing and giving thanks for the tremendous progress their sisters and brothers in the Church of Rome had made. Lukas Vischer, director of Faith and Order, can serve as spokesman, which indeed he often did during the council. "A new climate had come into being. The Roman Catholic Church had become a partner in the ecumenical movement. When the Council opened, hardly anyone would have dared to hope that such wide-ranging changes would come about."[27]

Sadly, Uppsala's radical hopes for a genuinely universal council have slipped off the WCC's and Faith and Order's agenda. These hopes received a brief mention in the postscript of *A Common Understanding and Vision of the World Council of Churches*, just before the Harare assembly of 1998.[28]

"A new climate had come into being. The Roman Catholic Church had become a partner in the ecumenical movement."

What remains on the Faith and Order agenda is the need to find ways of making decisions together. The preamble to the *Common Understanding* document says, "We are compelled by a vision of the church whose unity is expressed in bonds of conciliar communion which enables us to take decisions together and to interpret and teach the apostolic faith together, with mutual accountability and in love."[29] An earlier Faith and Order report, in 1976, admitted that "our present inter-confessional assemblies are not councils in the full sense" and wrote of the desire of member churches to "move towards full conciliar fellowship."[30] This needed to be based on a common understanding of the apostolic faith and mutual acceptance of baptism, eucharist, and ministry. The study of councils and the recent experience of Vatican II underlined the fact that in a genuinely universal and ecumenical council, all share communion together. In the World Council of Churches, this is not yet possible because it is not, as it admits, a council of the one church.[31]

The *Common Understanding* document also floated ideas about a future global forum. This subject will be explored in chapter ten. It is not clear in the 1996 documents whether the forum was intended as a replacement of the assembly or a supplementary form that would engage a wider range of churches, especially Roman Catholic, Evangelical, and Pentecostal, which for various reasons are not members of the WCC. All, I think, would concede that it falls far short of the original Uppsala hope for a genuinely universal council, a council more inclusive than Vatican II.

Looking through the Uppsala report again, and looking at my account of subsequent assemblies, I realize that much more ought to be said about relief work and Christian aid. Uppsala was especially concerned about Nigeria and Biafra. The discussion of this appeal at the assembly also provides an excellent example of how the churches are better equipped than many other aid agencies, because they have people on the ground who can not only say what is most needed, but also how aid can best reach those in need. Appropriately, as it would seem, the next assembly would be held in Africa.

CHAPTER FIVE

NAIROBI 1975

"Jesus Christ Frees and Unites"

Mainline churches in Europe, and more recently in North America, have been declining, but not as rapidly as those in Africa have been growing. In the space of a hundred years or so, countries like Lesotho have come to be described in the WCC's highly informative Ecumenical Prayer Cycle[1] as 91% Christian, compared with France's 70%, where churches were first established in the first century and are now declining. Yet any call for jubilation at successful evangelism seems overshadowed by political upheaval, civil wars, population growth, struggling economies, and the HIV/AIDS pandemic. All countries in Africa are now independent, but their desperate needs are too easily forgotten. That is why it was so important for the World Council of Churches (WCC) to meet in Nairobi in 1975, and for the Faith and Order commission to have met in Accra, Ghana, in 1974. My friend Martin Conway, co-author of *Introducing the World Council of Churches* (2001), said that at Accra, "the primary experience was of how much we have in common and how badly we needed each other in the common struggle for faith and obedience under the one Lord Jesus Christ." The same might be said of Nairobi.

Combating Racism in Southern Africa and Elsewhere

A worldwide fellowship of churches can help local churches in difficulty in many different ways. It can offer moral support in their struggles against injustice and help them feel less isolated. It can also, in its meetings and assemblies, practise what it preaches. Mainly white and mainly male assemblies like those at Amsterdam or Evanston are not best placed to tackle racism or sexism. By the time of the WCC's first assembly in Africa, in Nairobi in 1975, churches in the global South were having their impact, and so, too, were women. Men from Africa and India, often in traditional attire, were now more visible. So were the women. In view of what was happening in Southern Africa, the venue was particularly appropriate, but Nairobi was not the first choice. The assembly had been planned for Jakarta, in Indonesia. However, when it became clear that the presence of a large Christian gathering would only aggravate the problems this Muslim country was then experiencing, the venue was switched to Nairobi.

Nairobi at this stage of the World Council's development was the best place to be. Since the last assembly at Uppsala, WCC's central committee had established a special Programme to Combat Racism. "It was," said Allan Boesak of South Africa, "without doubt, the most controversial, but for Southern Africa's black people [like himself] the most courageous and decisive decision of the WCC." It would be tested for its effectiveness in many of the liberation struggles then taking place in Africa. Racism is not, of course, peculiar to Africa; it is just less easily disguised there. The assembly noted, "Racism, as a world problem . . . demands the churches' attention in other particular situations," and it mentioned the Korean minority in Japan, native peoples of North and South America, aboriginal peoples of Australia and ethnic minorities in New Zealand, black people,

> Nairobi at this stage of the World Council's development was the best place to be.

and migrant workers in Europe.[2] What is, or was, distinctive was the way apartheid in South Africa made a form of racism official government policy and, for some, official church policy. The separate development of black, white, and coloured peoples was said to be the will of God. Is it? A *World* Council of Churches can offer a broader perspective.

The Community of Women and Men in the Church

Sexism, too, is prevalent in various ways in many different places, so that no country and no church can serve as a perfect model of men–women relationships for others to follow. What became distinctive at the Nairobi assembly was having an entire session devoted to women's concerns and the decision to set up a four-year study on the "Community of Women and Men in the Church." On this and the racism issue, the WCC was responding to concerns raised in member churches. As US feminist and ecumenist Betty Thompson explains in a book about the major conference at Sheffield, England, in 1981, the culmination of the study project, "The Community of Women and Men in the Church is not just a subject for theological debate at global assemblies. This study has come out of the reality of local churches on every continent. It is no longer a 'for women only' issue but a concern for every witnessing community."[3] And, one could add, of every race and colour.

Nairobi was not the first assembly to think about women, nor was it the first to tackle what was sometimes described as "the race problem." Unlike councils of celibate bishops, such as Vatican II, most leaders in the movements that formed the World Council were married men – married, in some instances, dare I say it, to some very formidable women, well equipped to plead their cause. Years before Amsterdam, Henrietta Visser 't Hooft, wife of the first WCC general secretary, was arguing with the renowned theologian

Karl Barth about his expositions of Genesis and the Letters of Paul. Were women equal yet subordinate to men, as Barth tried to argue, even in his later *Church Dogmatics*? Partly at her prompting, one of the first acts of the Amsterdam assembly was to initiate a survey of "The Service and Status of Women in the Churches," which in turn produced one of the key textbooks on the subject. Its editor, Kathleen Bliss, was another very talented married woman. Bliss, like the Roman Catholic Barbara Ward, was very much a woman in her own right with a vocation of her own. She was joined in this project by Twila Cavert, member of the board of the YWCA in the USA and wife of Samuel Cavert, who was in charge of the arrangements committee for this first assembly, and by Sarah Chakko from India, soon to become the first woman president of the WCC.[4] What is important to emphasize is that such women could and did argue with the men, and put their concerns on the WCC's agenda. This they could not do at Vatican II. Barbara Ward, despite being an acknowledged expert on development, was not allowed to speak there because she was a woman. There are plenty of Roman Catholic women who long for the sort of open and honest debate that the WCC has helped to pioneer in the churches. In that debate, people like Kathleen Bliss and Sarah Chakko made the point that the ordination of women ought to be discussed, but it was not the only, and perhaps was not the most important, issue for the churches. Over 90% of the people in any church are lay people, and more than half of them are women. The general question that must confront all churches is this: Are women's gifts and vocations being encouraged and recognized not only in the churches, but also in the nations? If not, why not, and what can be done to help? More on this later.

> Are women's gifts and vocations being encouraged and recognized not only in the churches, but also in the nations?

Programme to Combat Racism

First, racism: 20 years before Amsterdam, Joe Oldham, the executive secretary of the World Missionary Conference at Edinburgh in 1910, who with his colleague and fellow layman John Mott was founder and organizer of more ecumenical initiatives than anyone else, wrote in 1926 a book entitled *Christianity and the Race Problem*. Oldham's book was quoted by the director of the Programme to Combat Racism in 1994, and by many others as well: "Christianity is not primarily a philosophy but a crusade. . . . In that temper we must approach everything in the relations between the races that cannot be reconciled with the Christian ideal."[5] This book was the first major study of race and had strongly influenced the development of subsequent campaigns against racism.[6] Hitler's racism, targeted so viciously against Jews and Roma peoples, put such convictions to the test in Europe, while in countries like South Africa, even before apartheid became official government policy in 1948, people like Gandhi were being shoved off pavements into the gutter just because they were coloured or black. Before the Nairobi assembly (1975), black people in the United States had been on the march, and one of their most famous leaders, Martin Luther King, shot dead. In England there had been race riots in Notting Hill, London. Sadly, despite so many good intentions and even a Special Fund to Combat Racism, in later years we witnessed genocide in Rwanda and Myanmar, and the massacre of Tamils in Sri Lanka and of native peoples in Latin America. The combating of racism is far from over. As Oldham said: Our common Christian concern is not to explain racism but to end it.

But in the process, WCC has had to ask a basic question: What approaches to combating racism are in line with Christian faith?

> Our common Christian concern is not to explain racism but to end it.

Theological Justification

Let's begin with theology, because racism in many different contexts, not just in South Africa, has often been defended theologically with a partisan selection of biblical texts to support the practice. God's people in the Old and New Testaments are a special people, "a chosen race . . . a dedicated nation, a people claimed by God for his own" (1 Pet. 2:9). At some stages in their history, God's people were forbidden to marry people of other races. Was this a precedent? Separate development of different peoples could be defended on the basis of Deuteronomy 32:8: "When the Most High gave each nation its heritage, when he divided all humanity, he laid down boundaries for peoples;" or by a somewhat partial appeal to Acts 17:26: "God created from one stock every nation of men to inhabit the whole earth's surface. He determined their eras in history and limits of their territory." And for centuries Christians argued that the Jews were only getting the punishment they deserved for their rejection of Christ, with appeal to a single text, Matthew 27:25: "His blood be upon us and upon our children." So Ham, cursed by his father, Noah, for some indiscretion became the ancestor of black people and of slaves: "Cursed be Canaan [son of Ham], most servile of slaves shall he be to his brothers" (Gen. 9:25). James Baldwin, who gave a keynote address at Uppsala, said, "I know that according to many Christians, I was a descendent of Ham, who had been cursed, and that I was therefore predestined to be a slave."[7]

The Nairobi assembly did not feel it necessary to refute the texts I have cited that are used to justify racism, nor did the following assembly in Vancouver. Instead, the assemblies replaced these texts with others. The World Council declared,

> Racism is a sin against God and against fellow human beings. It is contrary to the justice and the love of God revealed in Jesus Christ. It destroys the human dignity of both the racist and the

victim. We wish to add that it is a denial of the fullness of life, which is Christ's gift to the world, for in him there is neither Greek nor Jew, there is neither slave nor free, there is neither male nor female, but all are one. Christ on his cross tore down the barriers of hostility which keep people apart. (Ephesians 2:14–16)[8] [They could have replaced that citation with Galatians 3:27–28.]

The Galatians text refers to our "common baptism" into Christ and provides an example of how Christians can evade the authority of such a text. At the Synod of Dort in 1619, Calvinist divines declared that if you baptized a slave, you must set him or her free. So the solution was simple: don't baptize your slaves! This is cited by South African theologian John de Gruchy as peculiarly apt in view of the close links between the Dutch Reformed Church in South Africa and the Netherlands, in which the Synod of Dort was held.[9]

The Nairobi assembly noted a joint project with Faith and Order on "Racism in Theology and Theology against Racism" (WCC 1975). Later, on the wider question of how we interpret the Bible, the Faith and Order commission published *A Treasure in Earthen Vessels: An Instrument for an Ecumenical Reflection on Hermeneutics* (WCC 1998). We are all advised to beware that we approach scripture with our own prejudices and vested interests. The big question is how the same texts may be given an interpretation that may be mutually received.

Ecumenism without Borders

As one would hope and expect, those advocating mixed-race congregations in South Africa looked for support to mixed-race international ecumenical bodies like the WCC and international confessional bodies like the World Alliance of Reformed Churches.[10]

At different stages and in different ways, Roman Catholic bishops in South Africa, Anglican synods, the Lutheran World Federation, and the World Alliance of Reformed Churches condemned

Challenging the Right to Condemn Racial Injustice

In seeking advice from abroad, those advocating mixed-race congregations had to contend with a counter argument, which said that people outside South Africa had no business interfering with a nation's domestic affairs. The same issue was hotly debated in the United Nations, with British delegates exercising their veto against UN "interference" in the affairs of South Africa and what was then the British colony of Rhodesia. With the same argument, the way Nazi Germany treated Jews and Gypsies could be seen as a matter for the German government to decide. Or is there sometimes a duty for the international community to get involved in protecting the unprotected?

In 1999, the UN secretary general, Kofi Annan, asked Konrad Raiser, as general secretary of the WCC, to contribute to an international debate on humanitarian intervention. Like most leaders of the UN, Annan was a Christian, an Anglican from Ghana; he was asking the WCC to offer a theological and ethical perspective. By the time of the Porto Alegre assembly in 2006, the public issues committee could report that "the churches are in support of the emerging international norm of the responsibility to protect" in situations where a national government was no longer fulfilling its obligation to protect all people within its borders.[14]

apartheid. In their arguments they would appeal to theologians who are widely recognized in the *oikumene*: Aquinas, Calvin, and Bonhoeffer. A white theologian in the established Dutch Reformed Church, which officially supported apartheid and to which most

members of the government belonged, plucked
up courage to consult some of the best-known
contemporary theologians, including Karl
Barth, Emil Brunner, J.H. Bavinck, Hendrikus
Berkhof, Franz Lienart, and eight others. All
rejected racial segregation. Ben Marais' published survey, *Colour: The Unsolved Problem of the*

> **Our own denomi-
> nations may supply
> us with Bibles, but
> they also supply
> us with blinkers.**

West (1952), sent shockwaves through that church.[11]

Our own denominations may supply us with Bibles, but they
also supply us with blinkers. We only see the Bible texts they have
explained to us. We cannot see how others see us. Beyers Naudé,
as a young Afrikaner pastor in a wealthy Afrikaner suburb, did not
believe the harm done by separate development until someone took
him to see the slums and tenements in which black people were
forced to live.[12] He also discovered that his Anglican colleagues had
for years studied the race question and come to very different conclusions from those of his own Dutch Reformed Church. Prompted
by scholars like Marais and Keet in his own church, he turned to
theologians like Barth.[13] And as a Reformed churchman, he would
eventually be led with the World Alliance of Reformed Churches at
Ottawa in 1982 to see that any theological justification of apartheid
was a "theological heresy," not, as was claimed, good Reformed theology. No church wishes to be dubbed "heretical."

Mutual Accountability in the Body of Christ

Linked with the issue of "humanitarian intervention" in so-called
domestic issues of a nation is the question of mutual accountability, where one church claims theological support for its teachings
which other churches find questionable and at worst objection-
able.[15] Within confessional bodies like the World Communion of
Reformed Churches, the claim by a single church that "separate

development" is basic Reformed teaching should be agreed to by the wider Reformed community, or else renounced for what is at stake is the wider reputation of Reformed theology and founding fathers like John Calvin.

Resolutions on Paper or Action on the Ground?

As John de Gruchy, the noted South African theologian, pointed out, a major failure of the leaders of the churches in South Africa was their overconfidence in the power of resolutions and their tendency to believe that if the right word is uttered the task is activated. The Programme to Combat Racism (PCR) marked a new strategy – namely, active support for those who are actively engaged in struggles for justice and peace. Black Reformed theologian Allan Boesak described PCR as "the clearest sign yet of active, meaningful, ecumenical solidarity."[16]

The Question of Violence

But what if actions involve violence? In South Africa, and also in many United States and European congregations, the PCR funds were often branded as support for terrorist violence, despite the disclaimers that what was intended was humanitarian aid for liberation movements. Probed more deeply, few churches could claim to be pacifist and had resorted to war and violence whenever it seemed in a just cause and in their own defence. And even in South Africa, most white Christians underestimated just how violent the state was until the brutal facts were exposed by Sharpeville in 1960 and Soweto in 1976, including the murder of Steve Biko in police detention. Barney Pityana, a black South African theologian and former head of WCC's PCR, comments on the way one church after another joined the "litany of condemnation of violence," and adds that "the theology of non-violence and reconciliation sounded hollow when viewed against the churches' de facto recognition of an oppressive system." He welcomed the realism of the WCC, which acted on the basis that "where racism persists, violence and conflict are inevitable."[17] It was in response to the violent killing of nearly 70 protesters at Sharpeville that the WCC became more directly involved. With some local difficulties to be overcome, it sponsored an important ecumenical consultation with South African churches at Cottesloe in 1960 that even the Dutch Reformed Church engaged in. It was only after 20 years of verbal protests and consultations that a different strategy was adopted. John de Gruchy saw PCR as a challenge, as "it awakened South African churches to the fact that the time for non-violent change was running out." It roused a new sense of determination among the churches, he said.[18]

In 2001, the WCC launched a wide-ranging programme called the Decade to Overcome Violence, with the subheading "Churches Seeking Reconciliation and Peace." Such a programme was never more needed, as it followed the genocide in Rwanda in 1994, the massacre of Muslim men and boys in Srebrenika in 1995, and the attacks on the twin towers in New York and the Pentagon in September 2001.

Conscientious Objectors

The struggle in South Africa also raised the ethical question of the right to conscientious objection if you believed that your government's policies were unjust. It was an issue with which people in other nations were familiar. In the First World War, Britain imprisoned or fined men who refused to fight. In the United States, people like Robert McAfee Brown, a prominent speaker at Nairobi, could be penalized for opposition to conscription and the Vietnam War. John de Gruchy, in his *The Church Struggle in South Africa*, describes the "heated theological debate" in the South African parliament when the South African Council of Churches raised the issue of the right to conscientious objection. The names of Paul, Tertullian, Aquinas, Kuyper, and Barth were "tossed to and fro" as the churches' case was presented by the Methodist theologian and MP Alex Borraine.[19] Borraine would later be one of the chief architects of South Africa's Truth and Reconciliation Commission.[20]

Clarifying the Role of the WCC

On all the questions commented on above, it is important to emphasize that the real debates and the real decisions have to be made by local churches, not by people in Geneva, or by WCC assemblies and central committees. At best, what happens is that those on the ground ask the WCC for help. For some, what is offered will not be regarded as helpful. The government in South Africa regarded the WCC as a body infiltrated by communists and determined to cause chaos. Such charges will seem incredible to many of us, but they illustrate how the WCC, like its member churches, cannot take its own Christian credibility for granted. Respect can be formed only when opponents are prepared to meet. The South African government did its utmost to prevent such encounters.

Positive Legacies: The Truth and Reconciliation Commission

The apartheid debates helped South Africa and the wider *oikumene* clarify their thinking and responses to racism. They also bequeathed as their legacy the Truth and Reconciliation Commission and two outstanding black international statesmen/churchmen – President Nelson Mandela and Archbishop Desmond Tutu, who have been universally respected public figures for many years. Each engaged with the WCC. Tutu spoke at the Faith and Order conference at Santiago de Compostela, Spain, in 1993, and Mandela addressed the Harare Assembly in 1998. I quote parts of Mandela's address here:

When the World Council of Churches was established, the smoke was still lifting from a world shattered by decades of economic crisis and armed conflict, by the pursuit of racist doctrine and the violation of human rights. . . . The WCC helped voice the international community's insistence that human rights are the rights of all people everywhere. . . . To us in South Africa, and indeed the entire continent, the WCC has been known as the champion of the oppressed and the exploited. . . . When thirty years ago, you initiated the Programme to Combat Racism and the Special Fund to support liberation movements, you showed that yours was not merely the charitable support of distant benefactors, but a joint struggle for shared aspirations.[21]

It was good that Mandela felt no need to thank the WCC for establishing the Truth and Reconciliation Commission. It did not do so. He could claim that this was something Africans had established "through our own efforts." It was the product of soul-searching reflections by the former Nationalist government of F.W. de Klerk and the African National Congress, of which Mandela had once been a member. However, without wishing or needing to claim any of the credit, the WCC would know that several Christian people who had at one stage worked closely with the WCC were now giving a lead in their own country. They included Alex Borraine, architect of the commission, once active in the PCR and a former president of the Methodist Conference in South Africa; Archbishop Desmond Tutu, its chairman; and Brigalia Bam, once WCC secretary for women's concerns and then first woman secretary of the South African Council of Churches, later appointed by Mandela as chief electoral officer.[22] Tutu said that Borraine's account of the meaning of reconciliation, with its strong emphasis on facing the truth and accepting that reconciliation was a long process, was the best he had ever read on the subject. High praise indeed from such a reconciler.[23]

The commission also served as a model for Yugoslavia, Bosnia, Indonesia, and no doubt other conflict zones.

Massive Failure in Rwanda

"In a sad and little recognized irony, in the very month and year, April 1994, that the worldwide churches were jubilantly celebrating the first free, multi-racial, and democratic elections in South Africa, a few thousand kilometres to the north one of the worst instances of post Second World War genocide was being perpetrated in Rwanda."[24] Within a hundred days of April 6, nearly a million people were slaughtered by the army and even by their own neighbours. In retrospect, the Nairobi assembly could have foreseen such a tragedy in 1975, as dangerous conflicts between Hutu and Tutsi were already familiar. And how is it that in 1998, the scandal of Christians killing Christians seems to have left the WCC assembly in Nairobi speechless? If you had only the assembly report to go on, you would not know this genocide had happened not so far away and not so long ago.[25] General Secretary Konrad Raiser urged that the WCC must keep the memory of the South African struggle alive.[26] Equally so, but for very different reasons, we must never forget Rwanda. It teaches the churches many lessons.

Relationship between Church and State

With few exceptions, church leaders in Rwanda offered uncritical support to the government and enjoyed the prestige and power that rewarded their loyalty. In a country where most people were illiterate, the pulpit provided the best means of mass communication. But too often churches used their position to give out government notices rather than teaching the people as clearly as possible that in Christ there is neither Hutu nor Tutsi.

> . . . we must never forget Rwanda. It teaches the churches many lessons.

Ethnicity

Again, with a few courageous exceptions, church leaders accepted the culture that assumed that Hutu were superior and for that reason in power. Tutsi were inferior and officially not even human, but inyenzi, cockroaches. Ethnicity did not divide the different churches. It afflicted each church. Even church buildings that should have been places of sanctuary became killing fields where most Tutsi and their Hutu sympathizers were slaughtered.

International Responsibility to Protect

The churches failed to avert the genocide, and in many ways actively joined in the killing. The United Nations felt helpless and offered no assistance.

It is easy to blame the UN, just as it is easy to blame the WCC, while forgetting that the UN, like the WCC, can do only what its member states or churches support. The WCC's document *Nurturing Peace* recognizes this when it quotes the UN commander, Roméo Dallaire: "Ultimately, led by the USA, France, and the United Kingdom, this world body aided and abetted genocide in Rwanda. No amount of cash or aid will ever wash its hands clean of Rwanda blood."[139]

Vulnerable Women

The WCC study highlights the fact that in such conflicts, women are the most vulnerable. If we want to affirm human dignity, "we have to prioritize and affirm the dignity of women first." It urged strong support for victims of rape, when rape has long been tolerated as a weapon of war. Such violations of women's bodies are now made even worse by the prospect of infecting the victims with HIV/AIDS.

Community of Women and Men in Church and Society

Introducing the Nairobi plenary session "Women in a Changing World," Takeda Cho from Japan made the point she would be expected to make, saying, "In the life of the WCC, this is the first time that a plenary has been held in which women can speak clearly, fully, radically out of our concrete situations to the whole assembly." And they did. Dorothy McMahon from Australia urged the churches to give women more help in discovering their identity as women. Teny Simonian, an Armenian from Lebanon, spoke of the struggle for women's rights. Julia Ojiambo, a member of parliament from Kenya, told the assembly what it was like for a woman politician in a man's world. Una Kroll dealt with the sociological and psychological difficulties of working out the partnerships of women and men without either sex losing its distinctiveness.[28] Prior to Nairobi there had been a ground-breaking consultation in Berlin, "Sexism in the Seventies."

Granted that it is important for men and women from different contexts to try and understand and support "women in a changing world" to discover their vocations, there was very little in-depth theological reflection in this plenary. The assembly was aware of this, and the report on Structures of Injustice and Struggles for Liberation notes, "A thorough examination needs to be made of the biblical and theological assumptions concerning the community of women and men in church and society." They might have been hoping that as Faith and Order was to share responsibility for this study, more theological help would be forthcoming in relation to women's share in decision making, dialogue between those for and against the ordination of women,

> Julia Ojiambo, a member of parliament from Kenya, told the assembly what it was like for a woman politician in a man's world.

promotion of women's education, and encouragement for women theologians, as well as theological reflection on ministry to families and promotion of equal sharing of family responsibilities.[29] In short, enough here to challenge us all now, even 40 years after this assembly.

People in local churches do not always take much notice of what happens in assemblies even when they are well reported in the press. On this occasion, we in England did. A young man, Tom Wright, made a general complaint that the platform may sometimes shape and so control assembly decisions in advance, and thus that the assembly's style showed that the WCC could create its own structures of injustice. The assembly responded with "loud and prolonged applause." Wright later became Anglican bishop of Durham, and is today one of Britain's best-known and most prolific New Testament scholars. But general secretary Philip Potter was also applauded when he rejected charges that the platform manipulated debates on the floor of the assembly.[30]

It was a helpful reminder that WCC assemblies should set examples of good practice. They should also be more inclusive. Some progress had been made. At the Uppsala assembly in 1968, only 9% of delegates were women. At the Nairobi assembly, this figure was 22%. Why not 50%, given that slightly more than half the human race is female, and women outnumber men in most congregations? When this proposal was put to the central committee in 1981 after the consultation at Sheffield, England, earlier that year, it sparked wide-ranging controversy. Some objected to the WCC appearing to tell member churches whom they should appoint. There were also, says Betty Thompson in her report on Sheffield, "underlying questions of authority, biblical understanding, and doctrine."[31] By the Busan assembly in 2013, we can see much progress. The newly elected central committee went on to elect Agnes Abuom from Kenya as moderator of the central committee, the first woman to hold such a position, and four women and four men as presidents – a testament, as the report notes, to the principle of equal gender presentation.[32] At Nairobi, two women were elected to the presidency. That, too, was progress.

Churches in Solidarity with Women

The Nairobi assembly met in the United Nations' International Women's Year (1975), which in turn marked the start of the UN Decade for Women, 1975–1985. Once before, a similar international body, the League of Nations, had prodded the churches to follow its good example, and this was happening now. In 1987, the central committee agreed to a ten-year project, the Ecumenical Decade of Churches in Solidarity with Women (1988–1998). It was a very ambitious and adventurous programme. Living letters – that is, personal visits by men and women in member churches – to all 330 member churches was one of its best features. It was the first time all the member churches had been visited, challenged, and encouraged on a single major ecumenical theme: women![33] Paul once told the Christians of Corinth, "you are the letter that we need . . . a letter that has come from Christ" (2 Cor. 3:1–3): a living letter.

As good listeners and observers, the visitors quickly discovered and reported that women's priorities and major concerns differ from church to church and according to the culture and context in which women live and worship, but that the whole project had certain key objectives. According to one of its leading advocates, Mercy Oduyoye from Ghana and a deputy general secretary of the WCC, its general aim was to affirm the humanity of women.[34] "In this decade women are called to unveil their true womanhood, to offer their own self-definition of what it means to them to be women."[35] The churches are being called to help women do this. But alas, churches

". . . women are called to offer their own self-definition of what it means to them to be women."

are part of the problem. Hence, as women's groups, women were heard to insist that "we, too, are church"! One official objective became to empower women to challenge oppressive structures in their churches and communities.

Women can be oppressed in many different ways – from sexual abuse and violence and cultural customs like female genital mutilation to being overlooked and ignored. Churches aggravate the hurts and insults when they condone men's behaviour and abuse the Bible in defence of patriarchal attitudes and the silencing of women. A woman in Lesotho reported that if they tell their pastor they are frightened of their husbands, he will only tell the women to be patient. A theologian reported that as the only woman theologian in a group of men, she was asked to make the tea but decided instead to go home! When a group of women in Costa Rica gathered for a consultation, the men did take care of the children and the catering. Men can change, but not always. Letty Russell gained top marks at Harvard in 1957 as one of its first women theology graduates, but she was not allowed that distinction for fear of putting the men in a bad light. Russell, a Presbyterian, became one of the best-known feminist theologians. She took part in WCC events in Geneva in 1962 and in the Community of Women and Men consultation in Sheffield in 1981.

It is always hard to evaluate the effect of major programmes. Those involved were encouraged by the response of women and disappointed at the lack of response from the majority of men. The Ecumenical Decade of Churches in Solidarity with Women was too often Women in Solidarity with Women. The point was noted in the Women's Festival that preceded the jubilee assembly in Harare in 1998.[36] Sadly, the Busan assembly report on the Community of Women and Men noted that 30 years later, "most of the Sheffield recommendations in *Community of Women and Men in the Church* have yet to be achieved."[37]

Women's Ordination

Not all women wish to be ordained. This was made clear in the earliest WCC surveys by Sarah Chakko and Kathleen Bliss. But ordination remains a test case of whether churches really believe that women and men are equal and may be called by God to serve in any office in God's church. The WCC has kept the issue on the churches' agenda. Susannah Herzel, in her survey of the WCC's Women's department, suggests that "over the years the WCC may have done more than any other single body to promote and serve women ministers."[38] This was and remains no easy task. Even the widely read Faith and Order study *Baptism, Eucharist and Ministry* (1982) tries hard not to take sides in an ongoing argument, while expressing the need to work out the implications of Galatians 3:28 that in Christ there is neither male or female. "Though they agree on the need, the churches draw different conclusions as to the admission of women to the ordained ministry. An increasing number of churches have decided that there is no biblical or theological reason against ordaining women, and many of them have subsequently proceeded to do so. Yet many churches hold that the tradition of the Church in this regard must not be changed."[39] The commentary to the text also seeks a balanced view. Churches that ordain women "have found that women's gifts are as wide and varied as men's and that their ministry is as fully blessed by the Holy Spirit as the ministry of men." But others "believe that there are theological issues concerning the nature of humanity and concerning Christology which lie at the heart of their convictions and understanding of the role of women in the Church."[40]

One voice that should be heard here is that of Melanie May. She served as a staff consultant at the Ecumenical Institute in Bossey and relished the free exchange of ideas in that "Laboratory for Ecumenical Life."[41] But she is critical of how, in Faith and Order and other ecumenical discussions, women are too often regarded as one of the so-called non-theological factors and so not of prime importance.[42] Madeleine Barot had her presentation at the Evanston assembly deferred to the next day. As a result, busloads of women who had come to receive inspiration from her never heard her speak. Women were still expected to take second place. Perhaps an even bigger insult is the way in which women are sometimes regarded as an obstacle to church unity. Mercy Oduyoye cites the press headlines: "Archbishop Runcie and Pope John Paul II agreed that the ordination of women would prevent reconciliation of church families long separated over other reasons."[43]

Women's Theology

Women have their own perspectives, their own way of doing theology. This is something the WCC in its various projects has tried to encourage, though not always and everywhere.

One must not generalize about feminist theology, but one common feature is a strong emphasis on experience: what it means to be a Christian woman in a particular setting. The WCC has supported and encouraged groups like the Circle of Concerned African Women that Mercy Oduyoye founded, or Asian Women Theologians. Help from the WCC has been reciprocated, as such bodies have given strong leadership to the council through people like Mercy Oduyoye, Brigalia Bam, and Agnes Abuom from Africa, and Aruna Gnanadason from Asia. Nor should we overlook the impact, as at Sheffield (1981), of the Moltmanns, where Jürgen and his wife, Elizabeth, gave their respective male and female perspectives on the same theological issues.

Women find unsatisfactory the male assumptions and language which dominate in too many acts of worship. Did Christ only die for "us men and our salvation"? To that subject, highlighted at Vancouver in 1983, we now turn.

Herbert Wing (6) with Charles P. Taft, Reinhold Niebuhr and Henry P. Van
Dusen as they sail from New York to Amsterdam (1948) (WCC Archives)

Liturgical leaders process in Evanston (1954) (O.L. Simpson)

Vice-President Radhakrishan of India greets A.M. Ramsey, Archbishop of Canterbury, in New Delhi (1961) (WCC Photo)

Josiah Kibira, bishop in the Lutheran church in Tanzania, with unidentified church leaders in Uppsala (1968) (WCC Photo)

Indigenous people and delegates arriving at the Congress Centre in Nairobi
(John Taylor)

Youth delegates and women at pre-assembly women's event in Vancouver
(Peter Williams)

A procession in Canberra for the Justice, Peace and the Integrity of Creation programme (1991) (Peter Williams)

South Africa's president Nelson Mandela addresses the assembly in Harare (1998) (Chris Black)

The March to End Violence Against Women and Children in Porto Alegre (2006) (Igor Sperotto)

Teatro Ekymenikal from the National Council of Churches in the Philippines performs at the Mission plenary in Busan (2013) (Joanne Linden-Montes)

Willem A. Visser 't Hooft
General Secretary (1948–1966)
(WCC Photo)

Eugene Carson Blake General Secretary (1966–1972) (WCC Photo)

Philip A. Potter General Secretary (1972–1984) (Peter Williams)

Emilio Castro General Secretary (1985–1992) (Peter Williams)

Konrad Raiser
General Secretary (1993–2003)
(Peter Williams)

Samuel Kobia General Secretary (2004–2009)

Olav Fykse Tveit
General Secretary (2010–)
(Peter Williams)

Suzanne de Dietrich and Hendrick Kraemer at the Ecumenical Institute in
Bossey, Switzerland (date unknown) (WCC Photo)

Karl Barth (approx. 1920) (WCC Photo)

Sarah Chakko (1948) (WCC Photo)

Madeleine Barot (date unknown) (WCC Photo)

Robert Runcie (1990) (Peter Williams)

Kathleen Bliss (1954) (WCC Photo)

Yves Congar (date unknown)
(Unknown)

Mercy Amba Oduyoye (1998)
(WCC Photo)

Nikos Nissiotis and youth (1959) (WCC Photo)

Students at the Ecumenical Institute in Bossey, Switzerland (2014)
(Peter Williams)

Pope Francis and Olav Fykse Tveit (2017) (Francesco Sforza/Vatican
Photographic Service)

Agnes Abuom (2013) (Peter Williams)

Ecumenical pilgrims in Norway (Marcelo Schneider)

THE WORLD COUNCIL OF CHURCHES

Sixth Assembly Vancouver Canada July 24th to August 10th 1983

CHAPTER SIX

VANCOUVER 1983

"Jesus Christ, the Life of the World"

In the previous chapter, I gleaned much information about churches in Africa from the 2007 edition of the World Council of Churches' Ecumenical Prayer Cycle, *In God's Hands*. It also gives us many beautiful prayers to pray. Let us use them. Praying in most congregations, I know, has become too parochial. We pray for our own tradition, not the other folk next door. Protestants hardly ever pray for the pope, even though rumour has it that he is a good Christian and our best-known Christian spokesman. Vancouver, like every assembly, had many matters to deal with, but it made sure they were rooted in prayer and worship.

Worship and Praying for the World Church, and Including the Differently Abled

"Here we have no abiding city," said the author of the Letter to the Hebrews, perhaps reflecting on the harsh fact that the sacred Temple in Jerusalem was now in ruins (Heb. 13:14). In Vancouver, God's pilgrim people met each day in a big tent – , a "canvas cathedral," the report called it – that could be taken down and moved on.[1] It resounded with praise and prayer. "I have never sung so many alleluias or kyries in my life," said Jean Skuse from Australia.[2] A Roman Catholic from the Vatican Secretariat for Christian Unity, Monsignor Basil Meeking, described Vancouver as "a praying Assembly."[3] I was not there, but have been saying "Amen" to many of its prayers ever since, thanks to the beautifully prepared worship book which became one of the lasting legacies of this sixth assembly.[4] We can use it, as well as the worship books of all subsequent assemblies, whenever we divided Christians meet together in prayer. Aids to worshipping together have become one of the great gifts of the World Council of Churches (WCC).

This chapter will be shorter than its predecessors. This is not because worship and prayer are less important, but because the best and most important thing we can all do is worship God together, not just talk about it. "Ecumenical worship," if I may use such a controversial phrase, has to be experienced to be believed, and believing in the unity of the church often becomes credible the more we really pray together. US Methodist theologian Geoffrey Wainwright has written thousands of words about worship and taken part in endless discussions on worship in the WCC's Faith and Order commission and in dialogues, but he can still agree with a fellow expert on liturgy, the German Lutheran Edmund Schlink, when he

> Aids to worshipping together have become one of the great gifts of the World Council of Churches (WCC).

says, "members of divided churches find it much easier to pray and witness together than to formulate common dogmatic statements." In worship, he says, we face God and our fellow human beings. In dogmatic statements, we are merely talking about the proper way to witness and worship.[5] So, don't let us just talk about worshipping together, let's do it! That said, it is helpful to offer a word or two about evaluating the experience of worship and to describe what the churches have learned about ways of worship in the course of a century of meeting together.

Experiencing the Unity We Pray For

Janet Crawford of the Anglican Church in Aotearoa, New Zealand and Polynesia, and member of Faith and Order, was a keynote speaker at the WCC's first major consultation on worship, held at Ditchingham, near Norwich, England, in 1994. Reading her comments and the report of the consultation, we are left in no doubt about the importance of "experience." As a teacher of future ministers, she took a group of students to the WCC assembly in Canberra in 1991. Students found much of the theological discussion abstract and irrelevant, and were put off by the politics that often plays a part in nominations, etc. But, she notes: "Worship engaged [students] in the experience of being members of a worldwide community of faith, an experience which for some of them was both life and faith-changing."[6]

Much time and effort – and, one could add, creative imagination – is given to planning worship at ecumenical events. The result is, she says, that "for many people worship at WCC Assemblies and other ecumenical meetings is a highlight of their ecumenical experience. For many, ecumenical worship is a deeply enriching

> "Worship engaged [students] in the experience of being members of a worldwide community of faith, an experience which for some of them was both life and faith-changing."

experience of the worldwide nature of Christianity and of the diversity and richness of its ecclesial and cultural traditions."[7] We have even got used to being united in praise and prayer, and forget that what we take for granted today was impossible in the early years of the WCC. But how do we evaluate such experiences? Just a happy feeling, some might say. Let's enjoy each other's company and suspend our criticisms for another day. Or, and this is my conviction, because unity is a gift of God, not something we create, we should hallow these experiences as gifts. Christ makes us one, and this we can and do experience because Christ prays with us and for us, and our prayers for unity are answered.

Ecumenical Worship or Interconfessional Common Prayer?

But where ecumenical worship is not acceptable to all God's people gathered together in prayer, it ceases to be ecumenical. Ideally, such services should be prepared by representatives of the different traditions involved. This is difficult in such a diverse gathering as a World Council of Churches assembly. It should not surprise us or dismay us that not everyone finds it possible to worship together.

In the Special Commission on Orthodox Participation in the WCC, this was one of the concerns voiced by the Orthodox churches. They think of "worship" in terms of a liturgical eucharistic service of a type more familiar in their own tradition, and are happier with a more modest description of two patterns of praying together: confessional common prayer, such as Roman Catholic vespers or the Lutheran service of the word, and inter-confessional common prayer, often prepared by different confessions for an ecumenical event.[8]

Behind this concern are some criticisms of some ecumenical worship events that are more widely shared. Some of these were voiced at the Ditchingham Consultation in 1994, four years before the special commission was established by the Harare assembly in 1998. Thomas Fitzgerald (Orthodox and executive director of the WCC's Unity and Renewal Programme) made what may seem an obvious point that "Christian worship, even ecumenical worship, must always be worship of God."[9] Sometimes all our attention and devotion is focused on some current concern, like climate change or global poverty. Praise of God, thankfulness for what God is doing, and even invocation and petition may seem to take second place, almost as though we had no need of God or no relationship of obedience to his will. And there is also a reminder that all activities of a Christian council should be prayerful in the sense of being dedicated to God and celebrating his presence. So while Evangelical participants at Harare, with its theme "Turn to God, Rejoice in Hope," rejoiced and affirmed "the worship, vigil and evening prayers as moving and challenging experiences rooted in the Lordship of Christ," they regretted that the final commitment at the African plenary session did not mention Jesus once.[10] And I am sure many of us have been at services of prayer where we speak about Christ as though he were not there and praying with us. We need those like the Orthodox with their rich liturgies reflecting centuries of faithful devotion to remind us just how awesome is the prospect of daring to speak with God.

One Eucharistic Fellowship

According to the Constitution, "the primary purpose of the fellowship of churches in the World Council of Churches is to call one another to visible unity in one faith and one Eucharistic fellowship, expressed in worship and common life in Christ, through witness and service to the world, and to advance towards that unity in order that the world may believe."[11] The hope for becoming "one eucharistic fellowship" still eludes us. One senses a common feeling of

The hope for becoming "one eucharistic fellowship" still eludes us.

frustration in the protest of Emilio Castro in his general secretary's report at Canberra 1991, where he asserts,

The main aim of the ecumenical movement is to promote the unity of the churches in one Eucharistic fellowship. It is more and more frustrating that this has not been realized. We are able to be together in confronting the most divisive problems of humankind, but we are not able to heal our own history and to recognize each other within our common tradition. How can we expect to overcome divisions of life and death in the world when we are not even able to offer together the sacrifice of the Lord for the salvation of the world?[12]

Castro, as a Methodist from the Roman Catholic country of Uruguay, might personally have believed the solution is quite simple: that all the Lord's people are welcome at the Lord's table. But as an experienced ecumenical leader, he knew there are two major difficulties. First, the World Council cannot celebrate the eucharist, because the World Council is not a church. Second, even when we reach agreement on the meaning of the eucharist, as we did at Lima, and comprise a liturgy that reflects this convergence, the so-called Lima Liturgy, we are still not sufficiently united – especially in the eyes of our Orthodox and Roman Catholic sisters and brothers – to break bread together.

The first difficulty can be overcome by asking a local congregation to host a celebration of communion for the whole assembly. This was done at the first assembly, at Amsterdam in 1948. The authorities of the Niewe Kirk invited "all members of the Assembly who were baptized communicant members of their own churches to partake as communicants." The service was led by Reformed ministers assisted by ministers from other churches, and the pattern of receiving communion followed the Reformed tradition of being seated round a long table. For a congregation of over a thousand, this had to be done in groups of a hundred or so and took rather a long time, about two hours. Not everyone felt able to accept the invitation. On this occasion, the Anglican Communion and members of the few Orthodox churches then in membership abstained. Provision was also made at Amsterdam and at all subsequent assemblies for communion services according to liturgical rites of the major traditions. Practices varied as to whom was invited. At the Vancouver and Canberra assemblies there was an assembly eucharist using the Lima Liturgy.[13] It would be wrong to describe such a service as an experiment. Even for those who felt unable to communicate fully, it must have been a very moving experience to see the archbishop of Canterbury, assisted by two women ministers on either side, and four others from different churches, presiding. Most would be able to agree to the form of words and the structure of the service, for Max Thurian of Taizé had been invited and had agreed to compile a liturgy reflecting the agreement reached in *Baptism, Eucharist and Ministry*.

"Ministry" remains a major difficulty. The Reformed founders of the Taizé community, including Max Thurian and the prior, Brother Roger, solved the ministry problem at Taizé by inviting their Roman Catholic colleagues to preside and never doing so themselves. For some of us, this is only a short-circuit solution, evading issues that ought to be talked through.

Disagreements also follow from an unresolved argument: is communion a means of bringing divided Christians together or an expression of our unity and reconciliation as one church? One answer is "both," but for some that is being too simplistic.

Week of Prayer for Christian Unity

The Week of Prayer for Christian Unity, celebrated each year during the week of 18–25 January or alternatively at Pentecost, is the opportunity most Christians have to share in inter-confessional common prayer. The theme and prayers are chosen by an ecumenical group in a particular country and then adapted for local use by national councils of churches. Since the Second Vatican Council, overall responsibility rests with the Faith and Order commission and the Roman Catholic Pontifical Council for Promoting Christian Unity. The planning could not be more ecumenical. For 2016, Christians from Latvia reminded us that during the Cold War they experienced unity in their common witness to the gospel, even to the point of martyrdom, and that "today Latvia is a crossroads where Roman Catholic, Protestant and Orthodox regions meet," but no one tradition is dominant. As always, a particular biblical theme is chosen. In 2016 we reflected on what it means for God's people (1 Pet. 2:9–10) to be "salt of the earth" and "light of the world" (Matt. 5:13–14).

Three Christians from different traditions and different countries pioneered the way. One was Spencer Jones, an Anglican country vicar in a small town near Oxford.[14] He was joined in his concern for unity in 1908 by US Episcopalian Paul Wattson, whose religious community of Graymoor was received into the Church of Rome the following year. Jones reminded his Anglican colleagues of what the Lambeth Conference said in 1908: that "(t)here can be no fulfilment of the Divine purpose in any scheme of reunion which does not ultimately include the great Latin Church of the West."[15] Did this mean we should all "return to Rome"? Wattson seemed to think so; this became the emphasis in the Week of Prayer until another even more remarkable man, Paul Couturier, an abbot in Lyon, France, concluded that the focus of such praying was too narrow and exclusive. We should pray, he said in 1937, for the unity of the church in the way God wills and the means he chooses. That is what we have been doing ever since.[16] We no longer presume to know what the good Lord has in mind for us. We ask him instead! The World Council itself does not offer a blueprint for the unity we seek but, since the New Delhi assembly (1961), has offered various pointers, like the statement on mission and unity adopted at New Delhi,[17] *All in Each Place*, and now the Faith and Order document *The Church: Towards a Common Vision*.[18] "We have," says general secretary Olav Fykse Tveit of Norway, "a calling as a fellowship

> We no longer presume to know what the good Lord has in mind for us. We ask him instead!

of churches to express the unity of life that is given to us in Jesus Christ, through his life, cross and resurrection so that brokenness, sin and evil can be overcome." Thus, prayer for unity is linked with serious theological reflection on the unity Christ wills for his church and his mission to the world. We pray for a common vision.

Common Prayer for the World with All God's People

Today, many churches follow a Common Lectionary, based on a three-year cycle of Bible readings that since Vatican II have become part of the *Roman Missal*. They can also, since 1978, share in common prayer, week by week, country by country, using successive volumes of prayers from different lands and church traditions: *For All God's People* (1978), *With All God's People* (1989), and in book form and as an online resource, *In God's Hands: Common Prayer for the World* (2006). There can be no easier or better way of reminding people in some remote little village that they belong to the world church. And if today they are praying for Myanmar, tomorrow Myanmar Christians may be praying for them. They can also, through the introductory texts accompanying prayers for each country, learn a little about the people they are praying for.

All this is a healthy and much-needed corrective to a tendency for prayers in too many churches to become parochial, confined to the church leaders and members of our own tradition. In England

. . . a healthy corrective to a tendency for prayers to become parochial, confined to the church leaders and members of our own tradition

we pray for our Queen, not often for the secretary general of the United Nations, or even for the pope and the patriarchs and the WCC. Why not? "Prayer for unity should be a normal feature of church life in every local parish," said Emilio Castro in a helpful little WCC booklet entitled *When we Pray Together.*[19] In praying for unity, we are sharing in Jesus' prayer that "all may be one, that the world might believe" (John 17:21).

Partners in Life: People with Disabilities and the Church

In its assemblies and through special consultations, the World Council has made a bigger effort than many churches to help people with various disabilities feel fully included in all its activities. One discussion I shared in even challenged the language we use about each other. Might it not be better to say that we are *all* differently abled, rather than label some as disabled? We all have much to contribute as members of the same body. We are, said Lesslie Newbigin in a sermon on this theme, "Not whole without the handicapped."

This concern was again taken up at Nairobi in 1975 and then reflected on in some depth in a Faith and Order study, *Partners in Life: The Handicapped and the Church* (1979). It is a staggering thought that we are not talking about one or two people who may be blind or whose bodies may have been damaged by untested medicines or by disease, but some 500 million human beings, which is as many as belong to the WCC! "The unity of the family of God is handicapped where these brothers and sisters are treated as objects of condescending charity."[20] In 2016, the WCC's central committee, at its meeting in Trondheim, Norway, adopted a paper representing years of work by Faith and Order, the Commission for World

Mission and Evangelism, and the Ecumenical Disability Advocates Network. The title says it all: "The Gift of Being – Called to Be a Church of All and for All."

As in everything the World Council of Churches tries to do in its own meetings, the hope is that member churches will try to reform their own attitudes and practices, helped in some countries by legislation about access to public buildings, induction loops for those with hearing impairments, or large-print editions for people with impaired vision. Protestant churches, which place such a strong emphasis on "the Word," can learn much from other traditions, which are just as spiritual without being so wordy.

In the ecumenical journey, there were still a few people who joined the pilgrim route at Amsterdam and were now about to reach Canberra, the capital of Australia. One of them was Philip Potter, who was born in the Caribbean island of Dominica in 1921. I met him in Porto Alegre, Brazil, in 2006, his ninth assembly. He was general secretary of the WCC from 1972 to 1984. I wonder what he made of the ups and downs of the ecumenical movement over those years. He was usually too diplomatic to say! He died in March 2015 and had not been able to attend the Busan assembly a couple of years before, in 2013. Younger women and men must take up the baton. Ecumenism is more like a relay race, never a solo performance. Pilgrims help each other journey on.

COME, HOLY SPIRIT
RENEW
THE WHOLE
CREATION

WORLD COUNCIL OF CHURCHES
SEVENTH ASSEMBLY 1991
FEBRUARY 7-20 CANBERRA AUSTRALIA

CHAPTER SEVEN

CANBERRA 1991

"Come, Holy Spirit, Renew the Whole Creation"

Assemblies have to be planned years in advance. Events can take over and prompt spontaneous reactions that, with hindsight, could have done with more thought. My Baptist colleague Keith Clements, veteran ecumenist and one-time secretary of the Conference of European Churches, looks back on the assembly in Canberra as an example of the churches being too ready to speak and too reluctant to listen. Delegates felt compelled to tell the generals thousands of miles away in Iraq how the war should be waged. This, he insists, they were not competent to do. But any war, anywhere, makes it urgent to do some hard thinking about justice, peace, and the integrity of creation, and to do so theologically. That is why the assembly theme was a prayer for help: "Come, Holy Spirit."

War and Peace, Unity, and Renewing
the Whole Creation

The Justice, Peace and Integrity of Creation programme, which began officially at the Vancouver assembly in 1983, became a major theme at Canberra.

The assembly met in this Australian city in 1991, which was an eventful year. In the preface to the assembly report, general secretary Emilio Castro states, almost as an aside, "And, of course, Canberra will be remembered as gathering under the shadow of war." Indeed! The reference was to the first Gulf War, a response to Iraq's invasion of Kuwait. It naturally featured in the assembly message. "At a time of conflicts in various parts of the world, and particularly in the Gulf, we appeal for an immediate end to hostilities, and for a just resolution of conflicts in all countries of the world."

There had even been talk of postponing the assembly because of the war. "Others contended, however, that this was precisely the time when the world church needed to meet and speak a word of peace and hope."[1] The Gulf conflict was quickly over, with neither side being able to claim victory or establish a secure peace, only to be resumed ten years later. As I write in 2017, not just Iraq, but the whole of the Middle East is in turmoil. In 1991, Castro voiced what everyone could see: "the end of the Cold War has not ushered in a new era of peace."[2] Nor had it established a new world order. Twenty-five years later, disorder permits dangerous anarchies with unpredictable threats in unforeseen places – some, but not all, orchestrated by the so-called Islamic State. All euphoria at Canberra – because the Berlin Wall had come tumbling down (1989) and the Soviet Empire had collapsed – was short-lived. It was more appropriate than ever that the assembly theme should be a heartfelt prayer: "Come, Holy Spirit, Renew the Whole Creation." Even that would prove controversial. But at least Christians could sit round a table and argue their differences. Not so the wider world, awash with arms and remote-controlled drones.

Peace, Politics, and Unity

In one of several consultations that took place during the assembly on war and peace, a delegate from Hungary queried whether Christians and the WCC should get involved in politics. He was met with brusque response. One had only to read the Bible to see that prophets and disciples were constantly confronted with decisions about war. He could also be reminded that it was the First World War that prompted a Swedish archbishop, Nathan Söderblom, and the Ecumenical Patriarchate in Constantinople to plead for a "*koinonia* (fellowship) of churches" to match the newly formed "*koinonia*" or League of Nations in efforts to secure peace. Unity of divided churches and peace between the nations were intimately connected from the start. And this was confirmed when the failure of the League of Nations to secure peace meant that the inauguration of the WCC could not be held until 1948, after the Second World War ended in 1945.

England's archbishop, William Temple, saw the war itself as a battle that would affect the future of the ecumenical movement. His enthronement took place at Canterbury in 1942, in the middle of the fighting. In his sermon, he could not and did not ignore "the conflict . . . between larger and ever larger concentrations of power," the picture of whole cities in flames. But, he said, "there is another side to this picture. As though in preparation for such a time as this, God has been building up a Christian fellowship which now extends into almost every nation and binds citizens of them all together in true unity and mutual love." This "great world-fellowship . . . is the great new fact of our era." He added, "This is not the moment to say much about the war, but a German victory in

Germany's present mood, would mean the end of that ecumenical Christian movement and all the hopes connected with it. This is no guess. It is the declared policy of the German state and follows of necessity from its principles."[3] To support the point, Temple could remind his hearers that Hitler had taken Germany out of the League of Nations and had not permitted German church leaders to share in ecumenical conferences like those in Oxford and Edinburgh in 1937. Nazism and international ecumenism were incompatible. In more peaceful times, the Faith and Order theologians would conclude that concerns for the unity of all humanity put pressure on the churches to make their own unity visible. "Only the one Church can be the adequate counterpart of the one world."[4] But one senses a certain embarrassment at the fact that the nations were more anxious for peace than the religious leaders or churches were for unity. Hence the timely plea of Hans Küng, first expounded in 1989, that there can be no peace between the nations without peace between the religions.[5] Peace is not only a political issue. It is also deeply theological and hence a matter for the churches.

United Nations, United Church

It is no accident that the United Nations and the World Council of Churches (WCC) share the same birth decade: the 1940s. They were conceived for similar reasons and brought to birth by Christian people with a global theology they applied to both. Both organizations were guided by people who thought of being a secretary general (the UN's terminology) or general secretary (the WCC's terminology) as a religious vocation. To date, all the secretaries-general of the UN have been religious, and all of them Christian, except U Thant, who was a Buddhist. The WCC has, from the start, seen itself as acting in critical but supportive partnership with the UN, and is helped in this work by having an office in New York, not far from the headquarters of the United Nations. Secretary-general Dag Hammarskjöld once described his own role as that of a secular pope. Every assembly includes a greeting from the UN secretary-general, and on occasion the general secretary of the WCC addresses the UN. Paul VI became the first pope to address the UN assembly, in October 1965, and his successors have done so since.

To their credit, popes and general secretaries have used the opportunity to express the faith. For example, general secretary Philip Potter, when addressing a general session on disarmament in June 1978, declared that the basis of Christian action was faith in a God who in Jesus Christ wills life in all its fullness for all people, and that the earth be replenished for the well-being of all. He reminded the delegates that not far from the UN building, the Isaiah wall bears witness to the prophet's vision, which the churches still share: "They shall beat their swords into ploughshares and their spears into pruning hooks. Nation shall not lift sword against nation, neither shall they learn war anymore" (Is. 2:4). Pope Paul VI, invited by Buddhist U Thant to address the assembly, received a standing ovation. On this and other occasions, Pope Paul VI claimed to speak not only as a representative of hundreds of millions of Roman Catholics, but also on behalf of all Christians and non-Christians, believers and non-believers. He believed he had this mandate from Christ. On other occasions, we might wish to challenge such claims, but not when a pope is speaking "truth to power" and trying to be the spokesman for the majority of peoples everywhere who long for peace and have suffered so much in war.

Peace after Two World Wars: What Peace?

When Philip Potter, as general secretary of the WCC, addressed the United Nations Special Session on Disarmament in June 1978, he noted that while Europe and North America might be at peace, there

War Is Wrong, but We Are Not Agreed How to Make Peace

All those who assembled at Amsterdam in 1948 had lived through the war. Some, like veteran leaders John Mott and Joe Oldham, had also survived the First World War. "War" had to be on a responsible Christian's agenda. It was. "War as a method of settling disputes is incompatible with the teaching and example of our Lord Jesus Christ. The part which war plays in our present international life is a sin against God and a degradation of man."[6] But they regretted they could not say unanimously that war should never be waged as an act of justice. Can war ever be justified? Delegates would know of a long "just war" tradition that dates back to Augustine and Aquinas, but the advent of nuclear weapons made Augustine and Aquinas outdated.

Assemblies and committees of the WCC returned again and again to this theme, compelled to do so by weapons of mass destruction such as nuclear arms. Admitting something is evil can be a first step in doing something about it. Churches can help change the climate of opinion that makes weapons of mass destruction seem acceptable. If only they would! Speaking at a public hearing on nuclear weapons organized by the WCC at Amsterdam in 1981, Dominican theologian Edward Schillebeeckx said that all talk of there ever being a just war was passé. War is now so evil that theologians cannot possibly give it theological legitimization, he said. One could read these and all the other statements in a fully documented account, *Before It's Too Late*, published by the WCC in 1983.

had been 130 armed conflicts since 1945, most of them in the third world. He could have added that precisely because he represented a worldwide community of churches, we are intensely aware of each other's pains. Personal encounters with Christians from war-torn places bring this home in ways that reading reports and resolutions never can. Two women from Lebanon whom I met in Geneva were deeply touched when I knelt before them and apologized for the attitude of my own British government in prolonging the conflict in their country. And sensitive people in great and powerful nations like the United States will find a sympathetic hearing in WCC meetings that they might not get back home. Robert McAfee Brown, a Presbyterian from the USA and a leading speaker at the Nairobi assembly, had struggled with his conscience the more he heard of what his country was doing to the Vietnamese during the Vietnam war.[7] "The longer the war lasted, the worse things got. We were pulverizing the Vietnamese countryside with artillery shells and bombs from B-52s, and burning the inhabitants of the countryside with napalm, so diabolically effective that when it got into human flesh it continued to burn beneath the surface of the skin."[8]

In some conflicts, the WCC has helped to mediate a truce, as was once the case in the Sudan. In others, such as in Bosnia, WCC representatives visited churches caught up in the battles and helped the rest of us have a fuller understanding of what was happening, for there was, as they noted, "widespread ignorance of the causes of the conflict." Contrary to what was often reported, the religious communities had not instigated the war. Muslim, Roman Catholic, and Orthodox leaders all condemned the war but felt powerless to stop it

We are up against ideals and ideas. Success does not depend on military might, but in mobilizing consent to peace. That surely reassures the churches that they have a vital role to play. This was demonstrated in the case of the war in Vietnam. McAfee Brown was often critical of US secretary of state Robert McNamara, but came to respect his heartfelt challenge to the churches. He recalls McNamara explaining, "We face a depth of war fever in this country that is exceedingly destructive. Before we can end the [Vietnam] war, that attitude must change. . . . As the moral leaders of our nation, you clergy and laity must make it part of your task to help us create a climate of opinion in which we can de-escalate the war and bring it to a finish, without letting loose a political chaos that would tear the country apart."[9]

Historic Peace Churches

Mennonites, the Society of Friends (Quakers), the Church of the Brethren, and Christians with pacifist convictions may be a minority, but in today's ecumenical movement they punch above their weight. An inappropriate expression, perhaps, but a reminder that pacifists are not passive. They have had a hard struggle to be heard and have many martyrs for their cause. Now that nuclear warfare becomes unthinkable, we are more prepared to listen, a point noted by one of their most able spokesmen, Fernando Enns, a German theologian and active ecumenist. "It is apparent that the Churches that make up the World Council of Churches consider the Historic Peace Churches to have a significant contribution to make to their deliberations," Enns said.[10] The WCC assembly at Harare, Zimbabwe (1998), listened to Enns when he and others proposed "A Decade to Overcome Violence." They listened to Quakers like Eden Grace when she and others spoke of years of experience in resolving disputes in a less pugnacious, confrontational style, attending to the "sense of the meeting" and reaching decisions through consensus, rather than suppressing dissent by the tyranny of majorities. And even high-flown theological and ecclesiological discussions about the one, holy, catholic, and apostolic church have been challenged by the suggestion that commitment to peace and non-violence might have something to do with our vocation to holiness. Is the pedigree of ministers in the so-called apostolic succession the proper celebration of the eucharist, or the confession of faith expounded in the ancient creeds, or should ethics also be considered because of what Ephesians calls "the gospel of peace" (6:15)? Peace churches raise such questions.

Concern for Creation

Delegates to the Canberra assembly were deeply concerned about "the integrity of creation," which came out of the WCC's history of concern for God's creation and has carried forward in the years since the assembly.

When Pope Francis and the WCC's general secretary were invited to address the UN Summit on Climate Change in 2015, it was a clear recognition that the churches have a role to play in partnership with governments and environmental agencies who are convinced that care for this one earth is the major issue of our time.[11] But precisely because the world's churches are encouraged to be partners in a matter of global urgency, they have no need to go it alone, and indeed must not do so. Cooperating for the common good is all part of the mission of the WCC. Ecumenical Patriarch Bartholomew I of Constantinople, known as the "Green Patriarch," promotes care of creation and draws attention to the distinctive contribution the churches can make because of their faith in God the creator.

Ecumenical cooperation in concern for the environment and related issues got off to a good start with the Basel Convocation in 1989. This meeting was sponsored by the Conference of European Churches and the Roman Catholic Council of European Bishops' Conferences.

Cooperating for the common good is all part of the mission of the WCC.

For the first time since the Reformation, Roman Catholic, Orthodox, Protestant, and Anglican churches came together and marched through the city under the banner "Peace with Justice." The title itself was an echo of Psalm 85:10: "Love and faithfulness have come together; justice and peace have embraced." Basel itself was also symbolic. It is a city where three once-divided nations – France, Germany, and Switzerland – converge.

The attempt to act together globally at the WCC-sponsored World Convocation on Justice, Peace, and the Integrity of Creation (JPIC) in Seoul, South Korea, the following year proved much more difficult. Roman Catholics were late in being invited and took a whole year before agreeing. They complained that they needed more time to consider the various draft documents and proposals, and the WCC found it hard to cope with some of the alterations Rome wished to make. The result was that Roman Catholics were poorly represented at Seoul.

Nonetheless, the convocation was able to issue four covenants for action, including one that had climate change at its core. However, the WCC was short of staff and money and could not coordinate the vast numbers of local groups it had helped set in motion, or later implement programmes agreed at Seoul. In addition, its authority was questioned. It could not pretend to be the Ecumenical Council of Peace that Dietrich Bonhoeffer had once longed for and that the German scientist and peace advocate Carl Friedrich von Weizsäcker was advocating. Critics reminded the WCC that it had no authority to tell the member churches what to do. It was making no such claims, but that was beside the point. Another difficulty that has surfaced elsewhere is the gap in understanding between experts who comprehend the complex issues of climate change and sustainability and the members of a very mixed assembly of well-meaning but not always well-informed Christian people. This makes fully informed voting on complex proposals difficult.

All this sounds more negative that it needs to be. Marga Bührig, author of the critical study *Woman Invisible* (1987), was delighted that for a change there was a high proportion of women at Seoul. Less easily heard and, therefore, too often unnoticed are the voices of the poor and marginalized and inhabitants of tiny islands in the Pacific who already are the victims of the rape of the earth, to use an expression which chimes in with another big WCC and feminist concern about violence against women.

Deepening Theological Convictions about Human Stewardship of Planet Earth

Larry Rasmussen, who taught social ethics at Union Seminary in New York, is as good a guide as any to the way the WCC has helped develop and clarify our theological convictions about our stewardship of creation. He served as co-moderator of the JPIC programme. He is the author of a detailed WCC study, *Earth Community, Earth Ethics* (1996), and helps us see where we have come from as well as how as churches we ought to proceed.

If we had started from Genesis, we would have kept in touch with earth, air, sea, and soil as our common home, provided we did not mistranslate and misuse ancient texts like Genesis 1:28: "God blessed [human beings] and said to them, 'Be fruitful and increase, fill the earth and subdue it, have dominion over the fish in the sea, the birds of the air, and every living thing that moves on earth'." The British philosopher and statesman Francis Bacon (1561–1626) turned this text into a programme that in time would authorize the ruin of entire forests or the exhaustion of fish stocks. He argued that it was our human calling to "establish and extend the power and dominion of the human race itself over the universe."[12] According to this view, creation is simply there for our human use. It has no life of its own. Nor is there any conviction that we are accountable to God

Pacific islanders
of Nauru must
leave because
their homelands
have been pillaged
for phosphates . . .

for how we use or abuse creation. Generations of Christian thinkers delivered what Rasmussen calls "nature-irrelevant theologies" – nothing about the animals, nothing about the earth. But until more recently, the damage we could do was relatively modest. Now, at the touch of a button, we can destroy the lot. Now the Pacific islanders of Nauru must leave because their homelands have been pillaged for phosphates and they have nothing more to live on. So we are urged to reread ancient, sacred texts more prayerfully and listen to indigenous peoples who have lived in harmony with nature with tender loving care.

In addition to reviewing and revising how we have interpreted and acted on ancient texts, the following insights are emerging from JPIC consultations and discussions:

1. A holistic and integral understanding that care for the earth, concerns for peace, and convictions about justice must be kept together.

2. A holistic ecumenism. In contrast to UN and government approaches to development, the emphasis in the WCC is on "sustainable livelihoods."[13] Much can be made of the fact that *oikos*, home, is an integral part of the word *oikumene*, the whole inhabited world.

3. A eucharistic, sacramental approach to creation. In two major Orthodox consultations on the JPIC theme, this is a key insight the Orthodox have to offer: "Just as bread and wine are lifted up as an offering for the sanctification of the world and all people in the Eucharist, a sacramental approach to creation is needed for its reintegration."[14]

4. Covenanting for Justice. The *Final Document* at Seoul is subtitled *Entering into Covenant Solidarity for Justice, Peace and the Integrity of Creation*. However, there was much uncertainty

about "covenant." The Orthodox consultations and their theologians do not mention it. "Covenanting" is more familiar in my own Reformed tradition, where members of local congregations often bind themselves together to "walk together in the way of the Lord." The *Final Document* sets out to explain its basis in scripture beginning with God's promise to Noah after the flood: "Behold, I establish my covenant with you, your descendants and with all living creatures" (Gen. 9:9–10). It goes on to call on people to enter into an Act of Covenanting.

5. Concern for the marginalized. Though Aboriginal peoples constitute only 2% of Australia's population, they and their concerns were high profile at Canberra, helped in the process by Anglican bishop Arthur Malcolm, himself an Aborigine, who welcomed delegates to an opening plenary.

I was not present at Canberra, but soon after began to look forward to attending Harare. My role there was to write a report for Pilgrim Post, *the ecumenical journal of Churches Together in England. Even before the Busan assembly endorsed the metaphor of pilgrimage as a reference for ecumenical initiatives, "being strangers no longer but pilgrims together" had become our theme, as Roman Catholics now became active partners in our regional and national ecumenical councils and had their own insights about pilgrimages to share.*

TURN TO GOD

REJOICE
IN
HOPE

8th Assembly
World Council
of Churches

3-14 December, 1998
Harare, Zimbabwe

CHAPTER EIGHT

HARARE 1998

"Turn to God, Rejoice in Hope"

A lot happened in Africa since the last assembly met there in 1975. Robert Mugabe, erstwhile freedom fighter, had come to power in 1980. His country, Rhodesia, was renamed Zimbabwe; its capital, Salisbury, renamed Harare. After a long struggle, in which the WCC gave strong support, apartheid in South Africa had ended peacefully, and an amazing black leader, Nelson Mandela, was now president. How things change, and sometimes for the better! We had good reasons to "Rejoice in Hope" even as we made some tough decisions.

Mandela's Surprise Visit

None of us knew as we journeyed to Harare that Mandela would give a keynote address. He and another black South African, Archbishop Desmond Tutu, had become perhaps the most inspirational people on the world stage. Mandela's surprise appearance at the celebration of the World Council of Churches' (WCC) Jubilee marking 50 years since its foundation was a much-needed boost for delegates who had gathered with a feeling that the ecumenical movement was in difficulty – finances were at a low and the movement seemed to lack a common vision. The WCC might not have the momentum to continue much further into the future. For some, Mandela's unexpected visit remains the highlight of the assembly. It was certainly memorable. But there was another equally important dimension: the question of whether Orthodox churches would stay the course as part of the council.

Orthodox Concerns: Consensus Decision Making

Contrary to what many commentators think, the World Council of Churches, thanks to the inspiration and commitment of Eastern and Oriental Orthodox churches, has never been a purely Protestant body. It came into being partly in response to an encyclical of the Ecumenical Patriarchate addressed in 1920, "Unto the Churches of Christ Everywhere," urging the formation of a league, or *koinonia*, of churches because "it is the duty of the churches which bear the sacred name of Christ not to forget or neglect any longer his new and great commandment of love" – a love that had not been much in evidence in "the terrible world war which had just finished."[1] Orthodox representatives – including one woman, Irene Alivisatos of Athens – took part in the Faith and Order conference at Lausanne in 1927, and later in the Edinburgh conference in 1937, which agreed on the formation of the WCC. Some hesitated to join, or in the case of the Orthodox Church in Albania, were prevented from joining, but by 1994 it could be said that all Eastern and Oriental Orthodox churches were members of the World Council. Albania deserves a special mention. First because here, faith and faithfulness triumphed over all attempts to banish all Christian churches.[2] And second, because in Harare and subsequent assemblies and central committees, that church has been powerfully represented by Archbishop Anastasios, a saintly man you cannot help loving as he pleads with Protestants and others to be patient with the Orthodox. They think in terms of millennia, so cannot be expected to change their minds quickly, he says with such a gracious smile.

The Orthodox test everyone's ecumenical commitment, including their own. They have often voiced their unease, and sometimes their anger. At the assembly in Canberra they felt there was much to be thankful for: Faith and Order; work on the Renewal of Congregational Life; relief work through Inter-Church Aid, Refugees and World Service; the initiatives linked to the Justice, Peace and the Integrity of Creation programme. But! The WCC was inclined to forget that "the main aim of the WCC must be the restoration of the unity of the church. . . . Visible unity, in both the faith and the structure of the church, constitutes a specific goal and must not be taken for granted." In their disquiet, especially after a highly dramatic presentation by a Korean woman theologian, Chung Hyun Kyung, invoking the spirits of her ancestors and the victims of Hiroshima, they wondered if all those present were really Christians and if there were no limits to diversity. They would state, "We miss from many WCC documents the affirmation that Jesus Christ is the world's saviour. We perceive a growing departure from biblically based Christian understandings," even of the nature of the church itself.[3] At such times, they would find support in unexpected quarters, when, for example, they heard many Evangelicals saying the same thing. Many Protestant Evangelicals would say, and did say, the same.[4] These and some other misgivings to which I will refer in this chapter would come to a head at Harare in 1998, with real fears that unless other member churches in the WCC responded to their concerns, Orthodox churches would leave the WCC. The Orthodox Church of Georgia and the Orthodox Church of Bulgaria did leave. Others remained because other members of the WCC listened to their concerns and set up a Special Commission on Orthodox Participation in the WCC.[5] The report was formally presented to the central committee in 2001, but with appreciation that the desired mutual understanding between Orthodox churches and other member churches in the WCC requires constant attention. Following are some of the issues.

Ecclesiology and Orthodox Understanding of the Church and Her Unity

The WCC published a lively dialogue on this theme between a young Orthodox scholar, Peter Bouteneff, and a more experienced Danish Lutheran professor, Anna Marie Aagaard.[6] After they had read each other's reports, Aagaard came to a rather sad conclusion: "In my more bleak moments, I doubt that the Orthodox churches and the churches stemming from the Reformation will ever be able to set off together, so daunting is the task of even clearing the road" for the ecumenical journey. Both appreciate there is a problem, but describe it differently. For Bouteneff, the Orthodox start with a clear, God-given understanding of what it means to be church based on scripture and the tradition of the seven ecumenical councils of the undivided church – according to Orthodox understanding. They find it hard to square this vision with what he calls a "denominationalist" view of unity, which he thinks is the predominant Protestant view. Aagaard thinks she sees a way forward if we could all appreciate that unity and being church are always a gift

of God. She states, "My point is that 'church' is a constant trans-
mission in the created realm of God's forgiving and transforming
gift of grace."[7] But to receive this gift, and so become the church
that God creates, churches need to repent and ask for forgiveness,
from God and from other churches. But this, she admits, is what
so far churches fail to do. In my own words, no church confesses to
another church, saying, "Please help us and forgive us; we may have
got things wrong." Churches have annulled past anathemas against
each other, but perhaps Aagaard wants something more.

I warmed to Anna Marie Aagaard's approach, but then I am
not an Orthodox theologian. Her theology of the church is at this
point similar to Karl Barth's address at the WCC's first assembly
at Amsterdam (1948), where he spoke of the church as something
dynamic, an event, a happening, not some fixed, timeless institu-
tion. God brings people together, in a local congregation and in
meetings between churches. Unity looks different from an Orthodox and from a Roman Catholic perspective, where the starting
point is that we are already one. The one church, established by
Christ, "subsists" in the Church of Rome, as Vatican II tried to
explain; but because of churches which have separated from us, we
are not as "catholic" as God wants us to be.

The ecumenical movement challenges us all. But as Paul once
urged God's people in Rome, we who are strong must bear with
those who are weak. The Danish Lutheran Church represented by
Aagaard and the Orthodox Church represented by Bouteneff have
their own internal difficulties about unity. Who is strong and who is
weak? It is not that obvious, and was not obvious in Paul's account.
An Orthodox spokesman at the Busan assembly, Metropolitan
Nifon of Romania, was surely asking for help and support when he
explained, "Our greatest challenge comes from our own constituen-
cies. There are voices, and they are getting louder and louder, that
speak against the ecumenical movement, seeing it as a heresy the

Orthodox Church needs to confront." Maybe, as he suggested, this is largely due to "ignorance and a fundamentalist approach to faith," but it was easier for him to say that in an ecumenical gathering like Busan than among the Orthodox faithful back home.[8] Aagaard urges us all to read and reread Paul's Letter to the Ephesians. "There is church," Paul tells the Ephesians, "because God . . . blesses and chooses and brings everything into unity in Christ." Her own church, the Danish Lutheran Church, was not satisfied with the Joint Declaration on the Doctrine of Justification that had been agreed with the Roman Catholic Church. She was clearly disappointed. Views on justification by grace through faith need no longer divide us.

Ecumenical Worship or Common Prayer

In a previous chapter, I explained how, since the Vancouver assembly in 1983, much more attention has been devoted to the preparation of worship services at assemblies and central committees. Worship has always been important, as one would hope and expect in any assembly of churches, but at Amsterdam and subsequent gatherings one might invite members of different churches – and too often just the clergy – either to lead worship following a simple pattern of hymns, Bible readings, sermon, and prayers, or invite a host church or churches to provide services for those sharing in a WCC event. Vancouver's worship was much more imaginative and creative, with a real attempt to draw in the diverse traditions of the member churches. Such an attempt easily seems alien to Orthodox Christians. As Ioan Sauca, priest of the Romanian Orthodox Church and director of the WCC's Ecumenical Institute at Bossey, once explained to the students, Protestants often come out of church and comment on the service, saying, "Thank you for a lovely service," precisely because it is different. Orthodox revere the liturgy as something fixed and given and value it precisely because through the liturgy they are drawn closer to God. Other churches, like the worldwide Anglican Communion and the Church of Rome, have experienced major revisions of their service books and have had to come to terms with people who prefer *The Book of Common Prayer* (1662) or the Tridentine Latin Mass, one solution being to allow for greater variety in celebration.

Following the Harare assembly, where Orthodox challenges had come to a head, great care was taken at Porto Alegre to be extra sensitive. The assembly worship committee was chaired by an Orthodox leader, Metropolitan Professor Dr Gennadios of Sassisma, of the Ecumenical Patriarchate of Constantinople. He edited the worship book. The result, according to the editor of the assembly report Luis N. Rivera-Pagan, was that "most delegates wholeheartedly embraced the prayer gatherings held under a huge tent at the entry to the university and appreciated the efforts to ameliorate the tensions of past assemblies."[9] He explains: based on the experience of past assemblies, the worship committee took measures to prevent potential sources of conflict, including 1) carefully avoiding non-biblical, gender-inclusive language in reference to God; 2) impeding any attempt to force intercommunion or a common eucharist; and 3) naming the times of collective devotion "prayer" or "common prayer," thus avoiding what for some churches is the unacceptable concept of "ecumenical worship." But concealed within such a tactful and diplomatic description is the fact that for the Orthodox, "worship" means the Divine Liturgy of word and sacrament; this is something the World Council cannot celebrate, because it is not a church and its members are not united. Only a united church, such as the Orthodox Church or the Church of Rome, can celebrate

. . . naming the times of collective devotion "prayer" or "common prayer" . . .

the eucharist. When a WCC assembly has attempted to celebrate communion, as it did at Vancouver using the Lima Liturgy, it gets into trouble – trouble Porto Alegre later tried studiously to avoid.

Orthodox Challenges

When you meet great men and women who represent the Orthodox churches, you find it easier to accept critical comments they make. They love Christ's church and they love Christ. They care for the church's unity and ardently pray for the healing of her divisions. In the process, they face many challenges which are common to us all. In a moment I shall mention two people to whom the WCC and its member churches owe so much – Georges Florovsky and John Zizioula. But first let us look at these three: Nikos Nissiotis, Ion Bria, and Ioan Sauca.

Nikos Nissiotis, a Greek Orthodox theologian, is one of those brilliant people who could excel in many different areas, including sport. He was on the Olympics committee. He chose to dedicate his life to the ecumenical movement and the WCC. His early studies made him familiar with Protestant and Reformed theology at Basel under Karl Barth, and with Roman Catholic thought at Louvain. He was moderator of the Faith and Order commission, served as an observer at Vatican II, and was director of the WCC's Ecumenical Institute at Bossey (1966–1974). Ioan Bria is one of those self-effacing holy people who treats you as an equal. Only later do you discover that this friendly man was a pioneer ecumenical thinker, famous among other things for his book *The Liturgy after the Liturgy*.[10] He was director of the WCC programme on Unity and Renewal. Ioan Sauca comes, like Bria, from Romania. Studies in Birmingham, under Hollenweger, an expert on Pentecostalism, gave him that broad, "catholic" appreciation of the gifts in different tradition, that is such an asset for a director of Bossey, who is charged with supporting and interacting with students from all traditions and all continents.

In the years before Harare, there was a real surge of Orthodox activity. In the course of seven years, from 1975 to 1982, Orthodox church people were engaged in 12 seminars and consultations. As well as the topics "Orthodox Commitment" and "Contributions to the WCC," subjects dealt with included the service of women in church and society, preaching and teaching, theological education, diaconal service, and mission and evangelism. On none of these topics could any church stand up and say we have nothing more to learn and you, the Orthodox, have nothing to teach us. Some, like a call to respect the monastic life of constant prayer, presented a challenge to us all. Then, when the member churches were asked to consider a study document on the "Common Understanding and Vision of the WCC," the Orthodox held further deliberations at Chambésy, near Geneva, in 1995.[11]

Again, what comes through loud and clear is their conviction about unity: "We strongly reject any tendency which would turn the Council away from its fundamental vocation"[12]: the quest for Christian unity. And even more impressive is to hear or read about Orthodox theologians wrestling with a key question that is often evaded: what is the World Council? "What is the common understanding and vision of the World Council of Churches?" "What kind of fellowship are the churches finding in the World Council of Churches?" "An essential part of our fellowship is continuing to examine how we understand and experience this fellowship within the World Council of Churches." That statement and the preceding questions are set out by Raiser in his introduction to the "Common Understanding and Vision of the WCC" document, but some of the best answers come from Orthodox theologians.

"What is the common understanding and vision of the World Council of Churches?"

Metropolitan John of Pergamon, better known to many of us as John Zizioulas, author of the highly acclaimed *Being as Communion* (1985), first pays tribute to that Orthodox ecumenical pioneer, Georges Florovsky (1893–1979) before stating his own view, which is even more radical and constructive. Florovsky is described in *The Dictionary of the Ecumenical Movement* as "a universally recognised Orthodox spokesman for the ecumenical movement." He took part in the Faith and Order conference at Edinburgh in 1937, which helped prepare the ground for the WCC, was present and active in the first three assemblies, and was a member of the central and executive committees (1948–1961). He helped write the Toronto Declaration (1950), which eased the way for Orthodox participation by not insisting on any one definition of "church" or requiring mutual recognition of each other as "churches." But according to Zizioulas, his greatest contribution was to insist that the church could never be fully "catholic" unless it brought together East and West. And second, while churches may make their own rules about who was in the church and who was not – rules that are included by many churches as part of their canon law – there is also a broader, more charismatic concept of the church that recognizes that the Spirit of God is active beyond our borders. Zizioulas proceeded to take the argument further and say something very positive about the WCC. It is not just a forum where Christians can come and have a good discussion, valuable though that can be. It is not "a mere organizer of meetings." The fellowship in the WCC is an "event of communion" in the Trinity. It is in some sense a churchly body, or as he prefers to say, the WCC has "ecclesiological significance."[13] But to make this clear, it is imperative that the WCC keep the unity of the church at the centre of its life. It need surprise none of us that Zizioulas was a key speaker at the WCC Faith and Order conference at Santiago de Compostela in 1993. Before that he had had an important role in a major theological discussion in Britain, helping our churches to rediscover the "Forgotten Trinity." And it was Orthodox theologians like Florovsky who persuaded the WCC to make its basis in faith solidly trinitarian, not just Christocentric. Sound trinitarian theology and ecclesiology is a major Orthodox contribution and much needed for that reason, if not always welcomed.

Roman Catholics trace the pedigree of popes back to Peter, the rock on whom Christ founded his church, though Peter is never listed as the first pope. But it is the Orthodox who connect us with the earliest Christian communities. They link us with Antioch where, according to Acts 11:26, we were first called Christians, and Damascus in Syria, where Paul first encountered Christ. It was in a seminary near Damascus that the Orthodox held another major consultation as they prepared the way for Harare. Reading the report 20 years later, one is tempted to be envious of such a location at such a time. The host, His Holiness Ignatius Zakka I Iwas, Syrian Orthodox Patriarch of Antioch and All the East, spoke of the "spirit of love and tolerant co-existence between the different religions and denominations in this safe and secure country" and thanked President Hafez al-Assad for his impartial care for all. How times have changed! How much the peoples of Antioch and Damascus in the fellowship of the WCC, which they joined in 1960, now need our prayers. Because of Syria's internal strife, 11 million people have been made homeless, and the war goes on, and on.

Consensus Decision Making

As a minority in a largely Anglican and Protestant council, the Orthodox can easily be outvoted, so why listen to them? Because we are Christians! As Christians, we listen carefully to each other's grievances and are often helped by those who have the courage to voice them, knowing they might be unpopular for interrupting a debate and have their views dismissed in the vote. Parliamentary democracy may work for a parliament – though I am not convinced it always does – but is it the best process for a church? Even in the early days of democratic government in England, the Quakers, the Society of Friends, found a better way. Listen to everything that a brother or sister Friend has to say and then discern together the common mind, the "sense of the meeting." That, they believed, is more likely to express the mind of Christ than simply agreeing with the one who shouts loudest and cajoles your vote.

As was often made clear, even before the Special Commission on Orthodox Participation, that the Orthodox were not happy with the way the WCC assemblies and central committees do business. They were not the only ones, but they spoke up. Two practices affected them: majority decisions and voting. Though the Russian Orthodox Church is the largest church in the WCC, Orthodox churches are under-represented – and increasingly so, as more and more Protestant churches from the global South join the WCC. Is voting the best way to reach a Christian decision? In my own Reformed tradition, some of our best theologians stated, even before the WCC was founded, that to vote at church meeting was to admit failure. The ideal, as at Vatican II, was a unanimous decision, though that council did settle for a minimum of two-thirds majorities plus the pope's approval, and in practice achieved far more, even on highly contentious issues like the honour due to the Blessed Virgin.

The newly formed Uniting Church of Australia (established in 1977) had also reached the conclusion that old ways were not good enough for a renewed church. They could be hurtful rather than healing. So they sought advice from the Rev. D'Arcy Wood, president of the Uniting Church of Australia assembly from 1991 to 1994. As a member of the special commission, Wood inspired discussion on consensus and drafted the chapter

Is voting the best way to reach a Christian decision?

of the report about it. Ten years later, medical doctor Jill Tabart and others were able to offer their good experience of consensus decision making to the WCC, and offer their expert guidance to every assembly and central committee on how best to proceed, helped on several occasions by Eden Grace from the Society of Friends. There is no need here to go into details; they are well set out in Jill Tabart's book *Coming to Consensus*.[14] It is sufficient here to note what Gregor Henderson, general secretary of the Uniting Church from 1989 to 2000 and much-loved member of the central committee, writes in the foreword: Consensus decision making allows "more voices to be heard, creates more respectful listening and deeper trust in one another and brings about better decisions."[15] Fears that the WCC's "prophetic" voice would be muffled by the need to have everyone's agreement have not, I think, been realized, though it should be added that the WCC has also been sensitive to another criticism: that it is not the business of the WCC to tell the member churches what to do or say, but only to help them to come to a common mind whenever that is thought important. But the WCC is setting an example with this decision-making process, and many other churches, including my own United Reformed Church, are currently experimenting with the consensus process.

Some of us went to Harare feeling that this might be the last WCC assembly. Finances were tight, and there was much talk of stagnation. This Jubilee assembly would reaffirm what was said at Amsterdam: that "we intend to stay together." Pilgrim people, inspired by the Letter to the Hebrews, know that "here we have no permanent home." True. Our next tent would be erected in Porto Alegre, Brazil, on the Catholic continent of Latin America.

God, in your grace,
transform the world

World Council of Churches
9th Assembly
14-23 February 2006
Porto Alegre, Brazil

CHAPTER NINE

PORTO ALEGRE 2006

"God, in Your Grace, Transform the World"

Scottish ecumenist Norman Shanks had to admit that different churches had different understandings of grace when he explained the theme to the central committee in his role as moderator of the assembly planning committee. He would know that some of us query the verse in Cardinal Newman's best-known hymn, "Praise to the Holiest in the Height," which speaks of "a higher gift than grace." Can there be a higher gift, if grace means Christ? But like other assembly themes, this one was a prayer, and there is no point in asking God's help if we don't admit we need it! The subjects I select from all of the assembly agendas (not only Porto Alegre's) make it obvious that we did and we do.

Human Rights and Torture

The assembly in Porto Alegre, Brazil (2006), was the first World Council of Churches (WCC) assembly of the third millennium and also the first ever held in Latin America. Recommitment to the Decade to Overcome Violence (2001–2010) and discussion about programmes for global economic justice resonated strongly in the Brazilian context. Concerns for economic justice proved prophetic: just two years later, the world was hit with the worst economic crisis since the crash of the financial market in 1929, and ethics were at the heart of the debate among economists and ecumenical economic justice advocates.

Human rights were high on the agenda at the first assembly at Amsterdam in 1948[1] and again nearly 60 years later in 2006 at Porto Alegre,[2] when they were the subject of a vote of thanks to the WCC from the president of Brazil. At the following assembly, in Busan in 2013, moderator Walter Altmann, himself a Brazilian, reported that "the WCC received public recognition" for the project of secretly recording detailed accounts of torture and other such violations of human rights perpetrated in the long years of brutal military dictatorships from 1964 to 1985, in Brazil and elsewhere, in the hope that such atrocities, when publicly acknowledged, would never be allowed to happen again: hence the title of the project, *Brasil: Nunca Mais* (Brazil: Never Again).[3] Even when I visited Porto Alegre for the assembly, one of our guides told us quite openly that she had once been tortured. She might not know then how much the churches and especially the WCC had done to make the point that every human body has been affirmed as sacred because "the Word became flesh and dwelt among us." Something similar, though in slightly less religious language, was being stated by the United Nations, which had been founded only three years before.

The United Nations' Universal Declaration of Human Rights 1948

One reason why human rights were on the agenda of the first assembly was that they had just been affirmed by the Charter of the United Nations in June 1945. They were about to be spelled out in more detail in the Universal Declaration of Human Rights in December 1948, shortly after the Amsterdam assembly. It is a little-known fact that the WCC document *In Process of Formation*[4] was a major player in formulating key parts of both documents. One might hear their echo in the word "faith." The Charter begins with these words:

> We, the Peoples of the United Nations, determined to save suc-
> ceeding generations from the scourge of war, which twice in our
> lifetime has brought untold sorrow to mankind, and to reaffirm
> faith in fundamental human rights, in the dignity and worth of
> the human person, in the equal rights of men and women and of
> nations large and small . . . have resolved to combine our efforts
> to accomplish these aims.

Reference to torture is in Article 5 of the Universal Declaration of Human Rights: "No one is to be subjected to torture or cruel, inhuman or degrading treatment or punishment."

Contemporary historians tend to underplay the role of the WCC in international affairs, if they even mention it at all. And then it is too readily assumed that the churches were only interested in religious liberty and freedom of worship. This indeed was the focus of their attention in 1945, in a major study sponsored by the International Missionary Council that became something of a bestseller: *Religious Liberty: An Inquiry*. But this very thorough and scholarly study by a professor at Nanking University, M. Searle Bates, demonstrated in its 600 pages that freedom of worship raised a whole range of related issues: church and state, conscience, toleration, democracy, etc. All these had been under threat in the 20th century. Bates begins by declaring that "religious liberty is today denied . . . in most of the countries of the world."[5] He describes what had been happening in Russia since the revolution in 1917, in totalitarian regimes like Hitler's Germany, in Muslim countries, and in Roman Catholic Spain, "the only European country which does not enjoy religious liberty." But if here and elsewhere he is very critical of Rome and the teaching of various popes, he is also very ready to cite Roman Catholic commentators like Lord Acton who have more positive things to say. He quotes Acton's well-known words: "The most certain test by which we judge whether a country is really free is the amount of security enjoyed by minorities." Bates' balanced and ecumenical approach would encourage all readers to be sensitive and attentive to many other reasons why "we" – what the Charter describes as "we the peoples of the United Nations" – feel that some of our rights are being suppressed.

John Nurser takes up the theme in a WCC book with a similar embrace: *For All Peoples and All Nations* (2005). Its subtitle is *Christian Churches and Human Rights.* Anyone reading it will be in no doubt that the churches and the WCC were and are major players, and that a very strong lead was given by a remarkable US professor of education, O. Frederick Nolde. Born in Philadelphia in 1899, he became a key player in campaigns for religious liberty with the Federal Council of Churches in the United States and then as a director of the Churches Commission on International Affairs for its first 22 years (1948–1969). (The commission was related to the International Missionary Council and the WCC until the two movements were combined at New Delhi in 1961.) Nurser is anxious that we recognize Nolde as "the particular hero of this struggle" for human rights, for "he is now virtually unremembered in either the UN or the World Council of Churches."[6] Sadly, that is true. In *The Dictio-*

nary of the Ecumenical Movement we can learn about the "Ns": New-bigin, Niemöller, Niles, and Nissiotis, but Nolde gets only a one-line reference as spokesman for non-governmental organizations in discussions at the UN. Willem Visser 't Hooft is more generous in his *Memoirs*, but restrained in his praise. However, delegates at Amsterdam could read Nolde's 50-page essay, *Freedom of Religion and Related Human Rights*, in volume IV of the four preparatory volumes for the first assembly.[7] Later assemblies would never assume that delegates had time to read so much and be so well prepared to debate and decide. Nolde was one of many who established high standards of professionalism which later would too easily be dismissed as elitism.

Nurser says Nolde's great strengths were his ability to master the facts of a situation and a great capacity to work with people. Colleagues spoke of "his sharp and analytical mind, his warm and sympathetic heart, his tenacious and complete commitment, and his convivial and contagious spirit." He was "the articulate and informed voice of conscience."[8]

Nolde's other great gift was in discerning what Vatican II kept calling "the signs of the times," or better, the *kairos* moment. A whole host of factors combined to make this the opportune time for advocating human rights. In 1941, US President Roosevelt had spoken of the four freedoms: freedom of speech, freedom of worship, freedom from want, and freedom from fear. Like all US presidents, Franklin Roosevelt was a Christian, and so was his powerful wife, Eleanor.[9] Roosevelt died in office, but Eleanor, who had already championed women's rights, was soon to head up the UN Human Rights Commission. The end of the war in 1945 and the "liberation" of the concentration camps showed just what could happen if a nation or ruler became a law to itself and could torture and murder its own citizens at will. And there were a growing number of what became known as non-governmental organizations campaigning for the rights of their own members. The Commission of Churches on International Affairs, headed by Nolde, was joined by the Inter-American Conference on Problems of War and Peace, the Roman Catholic International Union of Social Service, the International Union of Catholic Women's Leagues, Jewish organizations, and various trade union groups. All accepted Nolde as their spokesman in negotiations with political leaders who were drafting the Universal Declaration of Human Rights. Mary Ann Glendon describes the scene: Nolde led off at a meeting with secretary of state Edward Stettinus "with a high minded exhortation, urging the USA, in keeping with its best traditions, to show leadership on this issue."[10] It did. And the whole process of setting up the United Nations and such a Declaration was nourished by what has been called a global theology and its practitioners, a belief in a world church and in world government organizations.[11] John Foster Dulles, a Presbyterian who was later secretary of state to President Eisenhower, is the most notable example of a person equally committed to the UN, human rights, and the WCC. He is also of ecumenical interest as the father of Avery Dulles SJ, one of Rome's best-known ecumenical ecclesiologists.

Alongside Nolde, another person who should not be forgotten is his colleague in the London office, Sir Kenneth Grubb. Grubb was never quite as certain as Nolde that the churches could have much of an impact on international affairs, but is full of admiration for Nolde and ranks Visser 't Hooft, the first general secretary of the WCC, as one of the ablest people he ever met. What he also admired about the WCC in its early years was that it took lay people like himself and Nolde seriously. Grubb, an Anglican, had a healthy suspicion of pompous clerics, having met quite a few in his time, not least in the WCC! His own good-humoured account, "Ecumania," is given in his autobiography.[12] Like Nolde, he served on the Commission of Churches on International Affairs for 22 years, up to the time of the Uppsala assembly in 1968. Long service and an office in New York enabled the commission to forge very strong links with the UN from its very beginnings.

The Universal Declaration of Human Rights was a remarkable achievement.[13] Forty-eight of the 56 nations that then constituted the United Nations voted for it. None voted against. Eight abstained, usually because they knew their own national policies were being challenged. Saudi Arabia could not accept the notion of equality in marriage. South Africa knew its own policies of apartheid contravened articles 1 and 2: that "all human beings are free and equal" and that everyone is entitled to such rights regardless of "race, colour, sex, language, religion, political or other opinion."

The abstentions raised the question, which has often been voiced since, of whether there can be such a universal consensus on human rights. Critics complain of foisting on the rest of the world Western, liberal, democratic, and Christian notions. It is true that the majority supporting the Declaration were the 37 Judaeo-Christian nations, but there were also 11 Islamic, six Marxist, and four Buddhist nations. None objected. Eight, as already noted, abstained. Insofar as the UN, like the WCC, is rarely in a position to be able to enforce its decisions, there is ample opportunity for dissent. What the declaration presents is a benchmark for measuring human rights and their abusers. As such, it offers international support to the work of bodies like Amnesty International and Human Rights Watch. As Christians, we will all surely wish to measure all our human judgments by the way of life revealed in Christ. The Evanston assembly (1954) welcomed the UN Declaration, but realized that Christians must go further. It stated, "The churches must . . . see in the international sphere a field of obedience to Jesus Christ. . . . The Church must seek to be the kind of community which God wishes the world to become."[14]

> **As Christians, we will all surely wish to measure all our human judgments by the way of life revealed in Christ.**

At the Harare assembly (1998), as part of the Jubilee of the Universal Declaration, the assembly discussed a detailed comment. Not least important is the strong emphasis on the Christian basis of human rights and the appeal to churches to make them a priority – for some had ceased to do so. It also lists specific WCC contributions to human rights since 1948. Some of these I deal with here.

Specific Human Rights

The Universal Declaration has some 50 clauses, and these still leave scope for others to be added. The WCC was reminded at its Porto Alegre assembly that it cannot do everything, and was urged to do less but do it better. It needs to recognize potential partnerships with other agencies that are better equipped to monitor and campaign on specific causes, such as prison reform. Some major issues, like apartheid and women's liberation, have been touched on elsewhere. Here I single out a few specific rights. Member churches and their delegates are always free to place new issues on the WCC's agenda while bearing in mind the limited staffing and other resources the WCC has at its disposal. The Consultative Group on AIDS, for example, involved 21 people from a number of different countries in developing a position, took two years, and included visits to many countries to test its findings before, with the approval of central committee, sending the document to the churches. Thankfully, nobody said "we can't afford to do this," but it all took time, personnel, and money.

Freedom of Worship

The way in which particular churches deny others the right to worship is an obvious example of an issue the ecumenical movement is bound to confront. For centuries, the Established Church of England, with the support of parliament, denied Dissenters and

Land Rights and Indigenous Peoples

When the assembly gathered in Canada 1983, it met some of Canada's indigenous people. Likewise, when it met in Canberra, it confronted the issue of land rights for indigenous peoples. From its beginnings, the WCC made clear that it is not a "super church," standing over and above member churches and their local congregations. So when Canadian churches were already supporting the rights of the aboriginal peoples in that country, the role of the WCC was to add the support and counsel of the wider church in the struggles of the indigenous peoples for recognition of their distinct identity and "their fundamental rights to their land."[21] The WCC, through its general secretary, would communicate the assembly resolution to the United Nations Commission on Human Rights and its Working Group on Indigenous Populations.[22]

The following assembly, at Canberra, Australia (1991), also issued a "Statement on Indigenous Peoples and Land Rights" with the subheading "A Move beyond Words." This is a much warmer and fuller statement than Vancouver's. It begins, "We have been graciously received by the Aboriginal people and Torres Strait Islanders who have shown great leadership and wisdom. We have worshipped together. They have shared their stories with us. They have shared their lives with us, their pain of stolen land and stolen children, poverty and oppression." The assembly passed a number of resolutions, including how churches might return lands once taken unjustly, oppose further exploitations, and respect sacred sites and freedom of worship for indigenous peoples.

Roman Catholics the right to practise their religion. Dissenters fled to Holland and then to the United States to worship as they wished. Huguenots were persecuted in France. Mennonites were persecuted almost everywhere. By 1948, some of this was old history, but not everywhere. When the WCC was invited to send observers to the Roman Catholic Second Vatican Council, it urged that freedom of worship must be on the agenda. It was. US Presbyterian theologian Robert McAfee Brown, who was active in the WCC and an observer at Vatican II, said, "this was our issue."[15] It was, too, since the observers' pleas found strong support from US Roman Catholic bishops, including the expert advice to the council of John Courtney Murray. Between them, they could argue that it was thanks to the US constitution that the Roman Catholic minority was free to worship in the United States. How, then, could Rome deny to others the freedom she herself was now able to enjoy? The resulting document, *Dignitatis Humanae,* states, "This Vatican synod declares that the human person has a right to religious freedom."[16] No one is to be coerced into believing what they do not believe.

The statement seems so obvious that it is hard for many of us to appreciate how radical it was at the time. The traditional Roman Catholic stance was that error has no rights. Those who are not Roman Catholic are in error and therefore have no right to "heretical" worship. The council was careful to insist that "this one and only true religion subsists in the catholic and apostolic church, to which the Lord Jesus entrusted the task of spreading it to all people,"[17] but it no longer denies that others have a right to differ in defining "the catholic and apostolic church" and what form true worship should take. Delegates to the Fifth World Conference of Faith and Order at Santiago de Compostela, Spain (1993), heard first-hand what a difference Vatican II made for Protestant life in Spain. Older

No one is to be coerced into believing what they do not believe.

people could still remember efforts during the Franco regime to assert that "Spain is one and Catholic" and had lived through "persecutions, imprisonments and exiles" for their Protestant faith. But since 1967 and again in 1992, they were now free to worship and were protected by law.[18]

What for people in Europe was and is an ecumenical issue is now in many parts of the world an urgent matter of inter-faith relations, aggravated by politics. The Busan assembly was very conscious of this. It issued a strong statement on the subject "The Politicization of Religion and the Rights of Religious Minorities."[19] Blasphemy laws "in several countries" are being misused against minority groups. "In countries of the Middle East region such as Egypt, Syria, Iraq and Iran, religious minorities live in a situation of fear and insecurity."[20] The United Nations was commended for its advocacy of freedom of religion or belief, but was also encouraged to do more. The assembly was also reminded that 2013 marked the 1700th anniversary of the Edict of Milan, which granted tolerance to Christians and all religions. What is happening today undermines such progress in mutual understanding and toleration. Such declarations often fall on deaf ears, but for those who are victims of persecution, these signs of solidarity may give the courage to persevere. In an assembly or central committee we meet face to face with those who are suffering for their faith, even if our love and prayers do not immediately alter their situation.

Freedom from Torture

Several assemblies have condemned torture. None, so far as I can discover, has ever said categorically that torture is always wrong. Without such a clear statement, it is very easy to denounce Latin America's military dictators or South Africa's apartheid government without admitting and confessing that when our own governments – for example, mine in Britain – practised or were complicit in torture, churches said little or nothing. Nairobi delegates said, "We must work for the abolition of specific denials of human rights, such as torture." They went on to observe how commonplace torture had now become.[23] The next assembly, at Vancouver (1983), also noted that "gross and systematic violations of human rights occur in most societies." It noted that the central committee in 1977 condemned the practice of torture and extrajudicial killings: "No human practice is so abominable, nor so widely condemned . . . but practically no nation can claim to be free of them."[24]

Churches were urged to denounce what is happening[25] – not, I repeat, to say that torture is always wrong. This is not just my personal lament, though I have raised the issue in discussions in central committee meetings and back home with members of Parliament. It is a sad fact that compared with other ethical issues, like abortion or same-sex partnerships, churches and theologians have given torture relatively little thought and have been slow to do so. One welcome exception is US theologian George Hunsinger's book *Torture Is a Moral Issue: Christians, Jews, Muslims and People of Conscience Speak Out,* based on a conference he organized at Princeton in 2006.[26] Professor David Gushee of Mercer University in the US offers "Six Reasons Why Torture is Always Wrong," the first being that "Torture violates the intrinsic dignity of the human being, made in the image of God."[27] Vatican II also appealed to the "image of God" in *Dignitatis Humanae* and elsewhere, without spelling out that torture is always wrong, perhaps because the council fathers knew that their church and the Protestants had once condoned its use. The theology gets better once we start admitting, as Gushee does, that torture also dehumanizes the torturer and erodes the character of the nation that tortures. The same point was made by Pope John Paul II in 1982 and is cited by Hunsinger in a lecture in Dresden in 2011: "Of their own accord, disciples of Christ will reject torture, which nothing can justify, which causes humiliation and suffering to the victim and degrades the tormentor."[28] US delegates at Porto Alegre, Brazil, confessed, "we acknowledge with shame abuses carried out in our name" and their failure to "raise a prophetic voice loud enough and persistent enough to deter our leaders."[29] For Hunsinger, it is an even greater shame that US churchgoers are more likely to support torture than those who do not go to church.

Rights of the Child

"All children have a right to be treated with respect. . . . We are called to welcome children as Jesus did." So said the Busan assembly, and it made this radical affirmation: "Children are equal members of the church and we can learn from children's understanding of God, their unconditional love for others, and their sense of justice." Very strong concerns were voiced about the facts that children are being exploited and are the most vulnerable in many of the world's crises.[30]

HIV/AIDS

The WCC has published more books on HIV/AIDS than on any other single issue.[31] Most books on the subject have been published since 2000, but the WCC was quicker off the mark in co-sponsoring a study with American and Canadian churches in 1989, resulting in the publication of *AIDS Issues: Confronting the Challenge*. A recent title, *Dignity, Freedom and Grace*, illustrates how, at least from a WCC perspective, HIV/AIDS is a human rights issue – not, as was too often assumed, just a consequence of personal sin and sexual immorality. "AIDS is a virus, not a moral condition." Not all agree. When AIDS first became a major issue at a WCC assembly, as it did at Harare, Zimbabwe, in 1998, the official response from Evangelical participants was, "We regret that the importance

"AIDS is a virus, not a moral condition."

of the family and of biblical sexual morality were little featured in the plenary, Padare or hearings."[32] ("Padare" describes the "open space for sharing and encounter.") By the time of this assembly, the WCC had begun its own serious research into the pandemic and was concluding that sexual morality was not the only issue. Nor was homosexuality. If one was to understand why, of the world's 39 million people infected with HIV, over half lived in Africa, one had to look for other causes. Gillian Patterson, author of an earlier study and editor of a 2016 collection of essays on the subject, blames poverty, which in turn makes some people, especially women, more vulnerable. One might die of AIDS in ten years' time but die of hunger tomorrow. So if a poor woman sells her body for sex, who is to blame? And sometimes it is the children of those infected who suffer. One mother had lost eight children to AIDS. Such facts were brought home to delegates at Harare. We were told that each week in Zimbabwe 700 people die of AIDS.

This is a human rights issue: the WCC challenges the churches to ask why some people are more vulnerable than others. Why is there still a "conspiracy of silence" about AIDS in some churches and in some governments?[33] Are medicines available and at reasonable prices, or are pharmaceutical companies exploiting demand and making vast profits? And does the Roman Catholic Church's official rejection of contraceptive measures like condoms aggravate the problem, or is total abstinence from intercourse outside marriage a realistic option? The WCC also asks and prays, as it did in the 1989 study: "May our response to the AIDS crisis lead us to create a more humane community at home and abroad." The 1997 study document *Facing AIDS* encouraged the churches to talk about the issue and offered some practical guidance. Don't talk about "catching AIDS," since AIDS is not caught like a common cold. Avoid describing people as "AIDS sufferers or AIDS victims"; instead, say "persons with AIDS."

My British denomination paid for me to go to Porto Alegre, and I am deeply grateful. I thought it was someone else's turn to go to the Busan assembly, and so did not ask to go. Now I regret not being there, but read on. Concerns about North Korea's nuclear ambitions have made us all very conscious of how vulnerable the seemingly prosperous nation of South Korea must feel. In Busan, one is not too far from Hiroshima and Nagasaki.

God of life,
lead us to
justice and peace

World Council of Churches
10th Assembly
30 October to 8 November 2013
Busan, Republic of Korea

World Council
of Churches

For more information: www.wcc2013.info

CHAPTER TEN

BUSAN 2013

"God of Life, Lead Us to Justice and Peace"

I was present at various central committee meetings where we decided on the theme for the tenth assembly. Some wanted a stronger emphasis on church unity, while others thought Christian concern for justice and peace was more relevant to the world as a whole. Through those discussions, the word "pilgrimage" emerged as a way of making clear that we were not just advocating a social programme that could just as easily be supported by the United Nations, but committing ourselves as churches to going to places of conflict and injustice – never too hard to find – and engaging in the process of being transformed into the pilgrim people of God we are called to be.

A Metaphor Becomes a Mantra

Delegates to the assembly in Busan saw first-hand the "wounds of a society torn by conflict and division," as the final message from the assembly said. Even so, the persistent search for unity on the Korean Peninsula became for them a sign of hope in the world. Delegates were conscious that this was not the only part of the world where people live divided by politics, conflict, and poverty. The recognition of the need for people to move together in order to come together became a dominant theme.

The metaphor of the ecumenical movement as pilgrimage came to life through assembly debate and subsequent reflections expounding on what became the guiding theme for the next years: "A Pilgrimage of Justice and Peace." Some of the subsequent reflections come from post-Busan issues of *The Ecumenical Review*.[1] There we learn that this is not just another programme, but a new way of describing what we, the member churches of the World Council of Churches (WCC), are all about. We have learned that pilgrimages can take different forms – such as a visit to a sacred shrine, like that of St James in the city named after him, Santiago de Compostela, in Spain, or to Lourdes, as a place of healing. But we need to make it clear that we are not just tourists who can say, "Been there, done that, got the T-shirt" and carry on with our normal routine. Real commitments are costly: they demand changes to our own way of life and that of our congregations. Justice and peace is the core of the gospel, says Dagmar Heller, former executive secretary of Faith and Order and professor at the Ecumenical Institute at Bossey. Dutch theologian Peter-Ben Smit sees being pilgrims together as an expression of catholicity. The final statement of the Busan assembly states: "To experience God's presence with the

> Real commitments are costly: they demand changes to our own way of life and that of our congregations.

most vulnerable, the wounded and the margin-
alised, is a transformative experience."[2] WCC
general secretary Olav Fykse Tveit says pilgrims
are open to what they see and are changed: "The
pilgrimage perspective makes us all humble." So we do not linger
too long at Busan, but move on.

**"We intend to
stay together."**

Moving On and Being Spurred On

In 1948, Christians who had spent most of the last ten years fighting
and killing each other came together in peace and told the world,
"We intend to stay together." We have. That was, and is, good news
for the world, for without our collusion, wars between Christian
nations could not have happened as they did in 1914 and again in
1939. In 2013 at Busan, after a long "ecumenical winter" – a phrase
Tveit used when he was elected general secretary – Christians from
around the globe made their separate journeys to Busan and told
the world, "We intend to move *together*." The world and its media
could not care less! But it should. When representatives of 560 million people from very different churches and cultures have found
ways of not only staying together but moving on, in a dangerously
divided world and in a country torn apart like Korea, it is good news
for all. We should say so! And give thanks to God for the gospel of
reconciliation as we join the pilgrimage of justice and peace! "This
assembly (at Busan) calls you to join us in pilgrimage." This chapter
is about moving on.

Ecumenism is a movement. Pilgrimage describes a journey.
Some participants became pilgrims together on
a peace train all the way from Berlin to Busan.
It took them three weeks. They were not in a
hurry. They spent four days in Berlin getting to
know one another and learning a little about

**Ecumenism is a
movement. Pilgrimage
describes a journey.**

What Moves the Ecumenical Movement?

Rereading one of the classics of the ecumenical movement, Ernst Lange's *And Yet It Moves* (1971), I was struck by his impatience. He had just been to a major Faith and Order meeting in Louvain and wondered why so few seemed to know where they were going or what they were aiming at, why there was so little enthusiasm and so much amateur discussion. But in calmer moments, he realized that different people come to such meetings with different ideals and different hopes, and they need time to sit round a table and talk. And he asks himself the big question, "Was bewegt die ökumenische Bewegung?" (part of the original German title: "What moves the ecumenical movement?"). He has seen enough and heard enough to know that despite everything, the ecumenical movement moves. The Unity Statement at Busan is not a repeat of what was said at New Delhi; the Mission Statement is also more holistic; and indigenous peoples are beginning to feel they have a place. Much of the leadership is now provided by women. But where are we going? Where are we moving to? Even Lange accepted that it is impossible not to give an unambiguous answer. We are not sure. We need guidance and so we pray, "God of Life, lead us to . . . " Where? To justice and peace? Lange reached his own conclusion: what we Christians stand for in the world is peace, God's shalom. "The ecumenical movement is a movement for peace."[4]

Korea. They stopped again in Moscow. "We spent three days with the Russian Orthodox Church," says our guide, Rilma Sands, a Presbyterian from Aotearoa/New Zealand. Had she ever prayed with the Orthodox before? Probably not. They moved on through central Asia, Siberia, and China, stopping in Beijing. On the border with North Korea they stared at the barbed wire and felt the pain of division between the north and south of the same country, symbolized later by a broken bridge, sign of a broken world.[3] At length they reached Busan, but for some the journey had only just begun. "To prepare for the next years as a people on a pilgrimage of justice and peace is now our task in this assembly," Tveit told the delegates. In the message from the assembly, we too are urged to move on.

Some would have preferred a more explicit church unity theme at Busan. A Roman Catholic colleague, Annemarie Mayer, who worked with the WCC as a consultant and is now teaching in Louvain, argues that the unity theme is implicit in the reference to "us" – "lead *us*" – the members of the churches, to justice and peace for the world.[5] Churches exist for the sake of those outside them, as England's famous archbishop William Temple once declared. Mayer reminds us that when Vatican II spoke about joy and hope, it was sure the joy and hope we have been given in our churches is a gift for the whole world. Its opening sentence is still worth quoting, and finds echoes in the message of the tenth assembly, *Join the Pilgrimage of Justice and Peace*. Vatican II speaks more theologically of "the Father's kingdom":

> The joys and hopes and sorrows and anxieties of people today, especially of those who are poor and afflicted, are also the joys and hopes, sorrows and anxieties of the disciples of Christ, for there is nothing truly human which does not also affect them. Their community is composed of people united in Christ who are directed by the Holy Spirit in their pilgrimage towards the

Father's kingdom and who have received the message of salvation to be communicated to everyone.[6]

Those at Busan wanted everyone to share their experience "of the search for unity . . . as a sign of hope in the world." They believed that "God our Creator is the source of all life. In the love of Jesus Christ and by the mercy of the Holy Spirit, we as a communion of the children of God, move together toward the fulfilment of the Kingdom. This assembly calls you to join us in pilgrimage."[7]

Theological Foundations for the Way Ahead

"A common call throughout this assembly [at Busan] has been to ensure that all WCC work has a strong theological foundation."[8] In the light of this plea from the assembly guidelines committee, I will endeavour to make this final chapter as theological as possible as I comment on various suggestions for the future of the WCC. Suggestions are drawn from the consultation "Ecumenism in the Twenty-First Century," participants in the Global Christian Forum, and veteran ecumenists like Michael Kinnamon, and from the leadership currently being given by WCC general secretary, Olav Fyske Tveit.

Prayer

Michael Kinnamon, from the Disciples of Christ USA, can justly claim, "I have devoted much of my ministry to the work of ecumenism."[9] He has been a staff member of Faith and Order, general secretary of the National Council of Churches USA, and author of numerous books, including *The Ecumenical Movement: An Anthology of Key Texts and Voices* (1997) and a critical study, *The Vision of the Ecumenical Movement and How It Has Been Impoverished by Its Friends* (2003). He therefore speaks with authority when he tells us that the best thing we can do for the ecumenical movement is pray. "I have long felt that the movement's single most valuable resource is the ecumenical prayer cycle . . . which invites the churches to mutual intercession and provides materials to help them engage in this spiritual discipline." He quotes in support what was said at Vatican II in paragraph 8 of the Decree on Ecumenism: "Public and private prayer for the unity of Christians should be regarded as the soul of the whole ecumenical movement."[10]

> "Public and private prayer for the unity of Christians should be regarded as the soul of the whole ecumenical movement."

Humility

Praying helps us to be thankful before God for those who have gone before us and to be humble about all our human ecumenical efforts for, as Kinnamon reminds himself and us, "God is the Chief Actor in this [ecumenical] movement." It is heartening how often "humility" is emphasized in recent ecumenical writings.

Olav Fykse Tveit set the tone in a lecture in Cambridge entitled "Unity: A Call to Be Strong or Humble."[11] Humility is built into the title of the Faith and Order text *The Church*. Although it reflects 20 years of deep reflection by what is still the most representative group of Christian theologians from around the world, it is not presented for our approval and applause as definitive dogma which must be believed. Rather, as it states in the final paragraph, "it is being sent to the churches as a common point of reference in order to test or discern their own ecclesiological convergences with one another, and so serve their further pilgrimages towards the manifestation of the unity for which Christ prayed." It is a step on the way, even if a big step forward, but it points beyond itself: hence the key word in the subtitle is *Towards* a Common Vision (emphasis mine).

Member churches were asked to respond as they had done for that earlier convergence text, *Baptism, Eucharist and Ministry* (1982), which became an ecumenical bestseller and created its own library of thoughtful responses. The church needs our help if we are to agree together what the church is and what we are called to be and to do.

Moral Discernment

Humility is also desperately needed in making ethical judgments. Quarrelling about morals might itself be immoral. It can easily be divisive. The Joint Working Group between the WCC and the Roman Catholic Church studied this issue in 1995 and produced the study document *Ecumenical Dialogue on Moral Issues: Potential Sources of Common Witness or of Division*. A current Faith and Order project is on moral discernment in the churches.[12] How can we agree on what to say and do together? As well as the humility and willingness to learn from each other, Tveit argues that there are occasions when the prophetic voice of the church must be strong and clear. Had that been the case in Rwanda in the 1990s, a million men, women, and children could have been saved from genocide. Just mouthing words like "reconciliation" does not make for peace. Decades earlier in Europe, the churches had not thought clearly about their attitude to the Jews. Hence, Hitler could initiate the terrible holocaust of six million of Christ's own sisters and brothers. Some Christians even thought this must be God's will, a just punishment for those accused of deicide, or murdering God.

Mutual Accountability

> How can we agree on what to say and do together?

Hopefully, all churches have moved beyond "polite ecumenism," when we simply compared notes but dared not challenge each other's attitudes to war and peace, church and state, fem-

inism and sexism, etc. Tveit made it the subject of his doctoral thesis, so we may expect to
hear more about its application throughout his
term as the WCC's general secretary.[13] He, too,
is accountable: "To be mutually accountable
means that I listen to the other to get insight
and wisdom, gained from life given by God."[14]
The Anglican Communion, in its Lambeth conferences, has wrestled with conflicting attitudes

> "To be mutually
> accountable means
> that I listen to
> the other to get
> insight and wisdom,
> gained from life
> given by God."

to human sexuality in its different provinces, with threats of schism
from those who are sure they are right and others are wrong. Paul
challenged those who threatened to divide the church over the issue
of food offered to idols and counselled, "Those of us who are strong
must accept as our burden the tender scruples of the weak and not
just please ourselves. . . . In a word, accept one another as Christ
accepted us, to the glory of God" (Rom. 15:1, 7).

Ecumenical Consciousness

If our own understanding of "church" does not stretch beyond our
own parish, local congregation, denomination, and church, we will
probably not be interested in the issues raised by Faith and Order
and other WCC documents. That is why it has always been a function of the WCC to "nurture the growth of an ecumenical consciousness"[15] in the members of all churches. I had forgotten this
was part of the WCC's Constitution until Simon Oxley, once a
staff member, made it the subject of his doctoral thesis. In a shorter
summary, he quotes what Oliver Tomkins said in 1952 (he served
as bishop of Bristol, England, 1953–1975) and Elisabeth Raiser said
more recently. Tomkins, born in China in 1908, told us: "By entering into a relationship with each other, we have already willed the
death of our denominations. The essence of denominationalism
is to suppose the sufficiency of denominations; the essence of our

> **"The ecumenical movement gets nowhere unless and until ordinary church people are involved . . . and carry the torch of ecumenism."**

covenant with each other is to deny that our denominations are enough."[16]

Raiser, a German ecumenical lay leader, contributes the chapter "Inclusive Community" to the latest volume of *A History of the Ecumenical Movement.* She states on the first page: "The ecumenical movement gets nowhere unless and until ordinary church people are involved in it, embrace it, and carry the torch of ecumenism." And she began with a quotation from a previous general secretary of the US, Eugene Carson Blake: "The ecumenical movement is a result of concerns of ordinary church people who find their ecumenical aspirations limited by church structures." As only the second general secretary, 1966–1972, Blake probably did not imagine that ecumenical enthusiasts might also sometimes find the WCC structures limiting. Two of the essays in the *Ecumenism in the Twenty-First Century* project make this point.[17] Professor Magali Cunha from the Methodist Church in Brazil reminds us that though most Latin American churches are not part of the WCC, "among ordinary people religious tensions and classical divisions are overcome without planning or structures in the struggle for Life and Human Rights." There is, she says "base ecumenism, in base communities." Hans Engdahl and Ander Göranzon give an example of popular ecumenism in South Africa. Tents pitched for funeral night vigils bring together Catholics, Lutherans, Methodists, and Zionists "doing this holy thing peacefully together, not worried by any theological scruples." What a pity! A pity if no one goes on to argue with the church leaders; this is what we have done, why can't it happen more often and "in church"? These authors quote the Danish ecumenist Anna Marie Aagaard, who said, "ecumenical theology must reflect a shared practice." I would add the British experience that often the practice is better than the theology! A Roman Catholic priest treats me as his brother in Christ and a fellow minister. This is not what Roman Catholic or Anglican doctrine says. When such rejections of others' ordinations are bluntly stated, as in the papal document *Dominus Iesus* (2000), even Roman Catholics are horrified and embarrassed by the reaction. Perhaps ecumenical consciousness is stronger than it looks. Or is it just that we have given up trying to change official attitudes and instead do our own thing? Many longed to make the widely supported German Kirchentags ecumenical, and succeeded in Berlin in 2003 with a joint Protestant–Roman Catholic event. But hopes for a shared eucharist at such a gathering were not realized.[18]

Ecumenical Theological Education

As we would all hope, those involved in theological education in different countries are trying to respond to the various challenges listed in the preceding chapters of this study. The detailed accounts provided by Dietrich Werner and Isabel Phiri of the WCC and their colleagues are given in two massive volumes of essays, covering in total some 2,000 pages.[19] Here I can give only a brief overview of their scope.

In South Korea, as delegates will have heard at Busan, the Protestant churches expanded very rapidly from a few thousand to nine million in the course of the last century, but now risk "deep stagnation." Teachers need more theological depth, for the churches are losing their credibility. Dietrich Werner, whom I worked with at Bossey when he was director of the Ecumenical Theological Education Programme for the WCC, is concerned about the "decay of ecumenical consciousness" in his own country, Germany; while in England David Hewitt, principal of The Queen's Foundation, an ecumenical college in Birmingham, welcomes the lead given by the Church of England in helping students to be better reflective practitioners.

The emphasis is not so much on changing the curriculum as changing the approach, on theological and pedagogical method. Here we should remember with thanks that the WCC once made the celebrated Brazilian educator Paulo Freire (1921–1997) famous for his *Pedagogy of the Oppressed* (1970), a consultant for its education programme.[20] Darrell Guder from Princeton in the United States put the emphasis on the formation of missionary communities, and would probably agree with Werner that much could be learned from earlier studies by the Dutch theologian Johannes Hoekendijk and his German colleague Hans Margull about the missionary structure of the congregation.[21] Tharcisse Gatwa from Rwanda thinks that Islam is growing in Rwanda, the Congo, and Burundi because of Christian failures to stand up for the poor against oppressive regimes, and warns against narrow-minded denominationalism. But on the continent of Africa as a whole, one of the most exciting developments has been the Circle of Concerned African Women Theologians. They are counteracting the Western missionaries' and African culture of patriarchy and male dominance. The members have to date produced over 100 books. Agnes Abuom, from Kenya, the first woman moderator of WCC's central committee, is a prominent member of the group. "Circle" aptly describes feminist ideals about leadership, reported in a WCC publication about an ecumenical symposium in Geneva in 1995, *In Search of a Round Table: Gender, Theology and Church Leadership*. Also from Africa comes the emphasis on nation building and human rights, as in Charles Villa-Vicencio's *A Theology of Reconstruction*.[22]

> **... one of the most exciting developments has been the Circle of Concerned African Women Theologians.**

All of the above studies illustrate various ways in which the WCC and its staff work with many different partners in the world church and with local councils of churches. Villa-Vicencio's book, for example, is dedicated to the "costly, formative influence in both church and society" of Frank Chikane, one-time general secretary of the South African Council of Churches. Often the WCC's role is humbler. As members of the council we are there to help co-ordinate and communicate what one church in one place can contribute to churches in all places; as we have all learned to say, together we share in God's mission to the world.

Global Christian Forum

Michael Kinnamon thinks the WCC is now less representative of the global Christian community than it was in 1948. This may be so. Since 1948, the majority of Christians have lived in the global South. Pentecostal, Evangelical, and various Independent churches have in many cases experienced rapid growth: these are the communions that are not part of the WCC, but are not necessarily to be branded as unecumenical. Are there other ways of expressing our commitment to unity in Christ? Certainly. The Global Christian Forum is one.

Those who have shared in a meeting of the Global Christian Forum tend to be enthusiastic about their experience. Others are not so sure it marks a way forward. This was clear when proposals were first discussed at Harare in 1998. At one point, the assembly report says rather coldly: "The proposal for an ecumenical forum received mixed reviews."[23] The assembly welcomed and encouraged the consultations that had taken place among those who expressed interest in sharing in such a forum. But it was also anxious that the call to make visible our unity in Christ should not be lost by offering the easier option of staying together as we are. A forum might supplement the work of the WCC; it could not replace it. In the WCC, committed membership of communions and mutual accountability are fundamental.[24]

".... new forms and paradigms are necessary" for the ecumenical movement . . .

Two people who have long been active in the WCC, Wesley Granberg-Michaelson and Huibert van Beek, both members of the forum committee, offered their own interim assessments after the first forum was held at Limuru, Kenya, in November 2007. Granberg-Michaelson is convinced that "new forms and paradigms are necessary" for the ecumenical movement, but pleads for honest analysis, creative exploration, and humble exploration. Huibert van Beek, secretary of the committee and editor of its first report, says, "Whether the Global Christian Forum is the appropriate answer in the long run remains an open question."[25] It is still something very fragile and provisional, and so in need of gentle support. Much of this support comes from the WCC, but is deliberately offered in a self-effacing way, so as not to deter any who might be suspicious of the WCC.

Though still too soon to give a simple yes/no verdict to Van Beek's question, we can attend to some of the points the participants at the second Global Christian Forum in Manado, Indonesia (2011), wish to share. First, they commend the practice of sharing each other's faith journeys. As one participant commented, "I was surprised to find that spiritually we were already one. This gave me sheer joy." All meetings, even WCC assemblies, might benefit if the journey to such assemblies would begin with the sharing of faith journeys that have brought us together. This is a real and practical possibility, as WCC participants now sit at round tables in groups of six or eight. All forum participants also affirmed the rich experience of relating to Christians of other traditions they had perhaps never met before. Even in some of the regional meetings that prepared the way for the first forum, it became clear that such encounters are not easily arranged, but bear fruit when they happen. Pentecostals and Roman Catholics in Latin America often ignore or resent each other, so not as many attended an initial meeting as was hoped. And in Europe, the Orthodox provided hospitality away from the Reformation disputes that can still afflict Protestant–Roman Catholic conversation. In his greetings to the first forum, Rowan Williams, then Archbishop of Canterbury, wrote that "the call to unity and common witness requires us to develop new conversations as well as build on the fellowship we already enjoy."[26]

Several participants repeated a warning that was long ago given to the WCC: Don't become institutionalized. Baptists warned, "We are concerned that an inclination could develop to institutionalize the movement, making it subject to authoritarian structures." Back in the 1960s, the WCC's Faith and Order commission engaged in one of its most detailed studies, *Institutionalism and Church Unity*, and even it concedes that institutionalism may be "a dimension of the ecumenical problem."[27]

Competing Convictions about Unity

When the Harare assembly first approved proposals for a Global Christian Forum, one of its concerns was that "participation by churches in a forum should in no way be seen as comparable to the ecumenical accountability and commitment of ongoing membership in the WCC."[28] This was one of the concerns that the central committee was asked to guard, for the point was also made that "there needs to be a clearly articulated distinction between the nature and purpose of the WCC and that of the forum."[29] But even when it said this, the WCC was in the process of reviewing its own common understanding and vision, as well as its relationship with its Orthodox member churches in particular. We are all being urged not to get stuck in our ways, but to move on.

Strong challenges to established ways of thinking were offered by a Pentecostal pastor at Porto Alegre in 2006: J. Norberto Saracco from Argentina. He offered us his own tradition's simple vision of unity that millions of Evangelicals sing every Sunday:

> You belong to the same church as me,
> If you stand at the foot of the cross,
> If your heart beats in time with my heart,
> Give me your hand. You are my brother, my sister.[30]

He admitted that "this ecumenical simplicity may be disturbing" for some, and that it "glosses over our real divisions," but he encouraged us to listen to "the ecumenism of the People of God" expressed in such a song, and made a case for a different approach:

> For evangelical churches, unity is not based on the recognition of a hierarchical authority, nor on dogma, nor on theological agreements, nor on alliances between institutions. We have to accept that this way of doing ecumenism has gone as far as it can. We know one another better than ever before, we have said to one another all we have to say, and we understand exhaustively the causes of our divisions. What is the next step to be? The ecumenical agenda must disentangle itself from the past and become open to the ecumenism of the future.[31]

There is no denying that much of what Saracco says is true. Let's move on! So, as was urged at Busan, join us – WCC members, forum enthusiasts, Roman Catholics, all our fellow Christians, join us in pilgrimage, and like those pilgrims of old, converse as we journey on.

Pilgrim Texts

As our conversations turn again and again to the scriptures we have in common, we can reflect on the Letter to the Hebrews and its pilgrim texts. They remind us, "Here we have no lasting city but are looking forward to a city with firm foundations whose architect and builder is God" (Heb. 13:14; 11:10).

"Only memory allows possibility," said renowned Bible scholar Walter Brueggemann.[32] May the ecumenical memory recorded in this book inspire us all to press on:

remembering those who went before us,
celebrating those who walk with us,
blessing those who come after us
telling again the story of the rolled-away stone.[33]

The Easter story, once told by the women, is the real source of our ecumenical inspiration.

Olav Fykse Tveit was encouraged that, immediately after the Busan assembly ended, he met a local delegate, Pastor Hurn, who told him he had just been meeting with other church leaders in Busan, and they had agreed to get together and form a council to address the needs of the people of Busan in a new way. Since then, many other places could tell similar stories, because they too are joining in the ongoing pilgrimage for justice and peace. Now that I have finished this book, I must see what else needs to be done. The pilgrimage of justice and peace embraces us all, whoever we are, wherever we happen to be.

NOTES

Introduction

1. Olav Fykse Tveit, General Secretary's Report. In: Erlinda N. Senturias and Theodore A. Gill, Jr. (eds), *Encountering the God of Life: Report of the 10th Assembly of the WCC* (Geneva: WCC Publications, 2014), 219.

2. Wesley Granberg-Michaelson, *From Times Square to Timbuktu: The Post-Christian West Meets the Non-Western Church* (Grand Rapids, Mich.: Eerdmans, 2013). Granberg-Michaelson was a one-time staff member of the WCC.

3. David M. Paton (ed.), *Breaking Barriers, Nairobi 1975: Official Report, Fifth Assembly of the World Council of Churches* (Geneva: WCC Publications, 1975), 15–16.

4. Norman Tanner (English editor), *Decrees of the Ecumenical Councils* (New York: Sheed and Ward and Washington, D.C.: Georgetown University Press, 1990), 818.

5. Constitution and Rules of the World Council of Churches (2013).

Chapter One: Amsterdam 1948

1. Willem A. Visser 't Hooft, *Memoirs* (Geneva: WCC Publications, 1973), 140.

2. Andrew Chandler, *George Bell, Bishop of Chichester: State and Resistance in the Age of Dictatorship* (Grand Rapids, Mich.: Eerdmans, 2016).

3. Willem A. Visser 't Hooft (ed.), *First Assembly of the WCC, 1948* (London: SCM, 1949), 28–29.

4. Karl Barth, *The Church and the Churches* (Grand Rapids, Mich.: Eerdmans, 2005 [1937]), 22–23.

5. *Lumen Gentium* (Second Vatican Council document on the Church), 8; *Unitatis Redintegratio* (Second Vatican Council Decree on Ecumenism), 4.

6. Visser 't Hooft (ed.), *First Assembly of the WCC,* (New York: Harper and Bros., 1949), 197–98.

7. Lesslie Newbigin, *The Reunion of the Church* (London: SCM, 1960), xi–xii. (This was the second edition of his defence of the Church of South India Scheme, revised in light of the creation of the WCC.)

8. *The First Six Years, 1948–1954: A Report of the Central Committee of the World Council of Churches on the Activities of the Departments and Secretariats of the Council* (Geneva: WCC Publications, 1954), 13–14.

9. "The Church and the International Disorder": Report of Section IV. In: Willem A. Visser 't Hooft (ed.), *First Assembly of the WCC*, 89.

10. *The First Six Years, 1948–1954*, 53–55.

11. Paul Ramsey, *Who Speaks for the Church?* (Edinburgh: Saint Andrew Press, 1969).

12. Robert McAfee Brown, *Vietnam: Crisis of Conscience* (New York: Association Press, 1967).

13. Keith Clements, *Learning to Speak: The Church's Voice in Public Affairs* (Edinburgh: T&T Clark, 1995), 22.

14. E.H. Robertson, *A Word to the Churches: Lund 1952* (London: SCM, 1952), 70–71.

15. Harding Meyer and Lukas Vischer (eds), *Growth in Agreement* (Geneva: WCC Publications, 1984).

16. *Baptism, Eucharist and Ministry* (Geneva: WCC Publications, 1982),

17. J. Philip Wogaman. (2011) *Christian Ethics, Second Edition: A Historical Introduction*. WCC Publications, Geneva, 298

18. Robertson, *A Word to the Churches*, 30.

19. Charles West, *Communism and the Theologians* (London: SCM, 1958); "The Church in Post Marxist Society." In: Frank D. Macchia and Paul S. Chung (eds), *Theology between East and West: A Radical Heritage* (Eugene, Ore.: Cascade Books, 2002), 297–316.

Chapter Two: Evanston 1954

1. Yves Congar, *Journal* (3 May 1964).

2. Council of the Evangelical Church in Germany, *Declaration to the Representatives of the World Council of Churches* (19 October 1945).

3. Wolfgang Gerlach, *The Confessing Church and the Persecution of the Jews*, Hamburg Thesis 1970 (Lincoln, Neb.: University of Nebraska, 2000).

4. Ivan Kershaw, *Popular Opinion and Political Dissent in the Third Reich* (Oxford: Clarendon Press, 1983), viii.

5. Irving Greenberg, Simon Herman and Yehuda Bauer (eds), *Interpreting the Holocaust for Future Generations* (New York: Memorial Foundation for Jewish Culture, 1974), 19–20.

6. Haim Chertok, *He Also Spoke as a Jew: The Life of James Parkes* (London: Valentine Mitchell, 2006), 290.

7. Willem A. Visser 't Hooft (ed.), *The New Delhi Report: The Third Assembly of the WCC, 1961* (London: SCM, 1962), 42, 148.

8. Donald W. Norwood, *Reforming Rome: Karl Barth and Vatican II* (Grand Rapids, Mich.: Eerdmans, 2015), 229.

9. Ibid., 225.

10. Gerhart Riegner, *Never Despair* (Chicago: Ivan Dee, 2006), 15–126; Willem Visser 't Hooft, *Memoirs* (London: SCM, 1973), 168.

11. Karl Barth, *Church Dogmatics, IV.3.2: The Doctrine of Reconciliation, Study Edition* (New York: T&T Clark, 1959), 192.

12. *Christ and the Church*, Faith and Order Paper 38 (Geneva: WCC, 1925), 40.

13. Paul S. Minear, *Images of the Church in the New Testament* (Louisville: Westminster John Knox, 2004 [1960]).

14. Geza Vermes, *The Real Jesus: Then and Now* (Minneapolis, Minn.: Fortress Press, 2010), 33.

15. Willem A. Visser 't Hooft (ed.), *The Evanston Report: The Second Assembly of the WCC, 1954* (London: SCM, 1955), 327–28; Assembly Debate, 72–79.

16. Visser 't Hooft (ed.), *The Evanston Report*, 74.

17. Luis N. Rivera-Pagan (ed.), *God, in Your Grace . . .: Official Report of the Ninth Assembly of the WCC* (Geneva: WCC Publications, 2007), 382–83.

18. Walter Müller Romheld, "Suzanne de Diétrich," in *Dictionary of the Ecumenical Movement*, 2d ed., ed. Nicholas Lossky et al. (Geneva: WCC Publications, 2002), 326, quoting an associate.

19. Werner Hühne, *A Man to Be Reckoned With: The Story of Reinold von Thadden-Trieglaff, the Founder of the German Kirchentag* (London: SCM, 1962).

20. Willem A. Visser 't Hooft (ed.), *First Assembly of the WCC, 1948* (London: SCM, 1949).

21. Visser 't Hooft (ed.), *The New Delhi Report*.

22. Visser 't Hooft (ed.), *The Evanston Report*, 90; E.H. Robertson, *An Account of the Third World Conference on Faith and Order, August 1952* (London: SCM, 1952).

Chapter Three: New Delhi 1961

1. Willem A. Visser't Hooft, *The New Delhi Report: The Third Assembly of the WCC, 1961* (London: SCM, 1962).116.

2. Kirsteen Kim and Andrew Anderson (eds), *Edinburgh 2010: Mission Today and Tomorrow* (Oxford: Regnum Books, 2011). (One of a series of books about the centenary of Edinburgh 1910.)

3. Cited in Brian Stanley, *The World Missionary Conference, Edinburgh 1910* (Grand Rapids, Mich.: Eerdmans, 2009), 103; William Richey Hogg, *Ecumen-*

ical Foundations: A History of the International Missionary Council (New York: Harper Brothers, 1952).

4. Stanley, *The World Missionary Conference, Edinburgh 1910*, 310ff.

5. David J. Bosch, *Transforming Mission: Paradigm Shifts in the Theology of Mission* (Maryknoll, N.Y.: Orbis, 1991).

6. Norman Goodall, *Ecumenical Progress: A Decade of Change in the Ecumenical Movement 1961–1971* (Oxford: Oxford University Press, 1972), 30.

7. Oliver Tomkins, "Mott, John R.," *Dictionary of the Ecumenical Movement*, ed. Nicholas Lossky et al., 2d ed. (Geneva: WCC Publications, 2002), 799.

8. Vinay Samuel and Chris Sugden (eds), *AD 2000 and Beyond: A Mission Agenda. A Festschrift for John Stott's 70th Birthday* (Oxford: Regnum, 1991), xi.

9. "A Jubilee Call: A Letter to the WCC by Evangelical Participants at Harare." In: Diane Kessler (ed.), *Together on the Way: Official Report of the Eighth Assembly of the WCC* (Geneva: WCC Publications, 1999), 265–71.

10. Thomas Wieser (ed.), *Planning for Mission: Working Paper on the New Quest for Missionary Communities* (London: Epworth Press, 1966), 220; *The Church for Others, and the Church for the World: A Quest for Structures for Missionary Congregations*. Final report of the Western European Working Group and North American Working Group of the Department on Studies in Evangelism (Geneva: WCC Publications, 1967).

11. Gerhard Linn (ed.), *Hear What the Spirit Says to the Churches* (Geneva: WCC Publications, 1994).

12. Lesslie Newbigin. "Mission in Six Continents." In: Harold E. Fey (ed.), *A History of the Ecumenical Movement, Vol. 2, 1948–1968* (Geneva: WCC Publications, 1970/1986), 171–97.

13. This is the title of a hymn by Edward Joseph Burns.

14. Kirsteem Kim, "Globalization of Protestant Movements since the 1960's," *The Ecumenical Review* 63:2 (2011): 136–47.

15. Harvey T. Hoekstra, *Evangelism in Eclipse: World Mission and the World Council of Churches* (Exeter: Paternoster Press, 1979); Norman Goodall, *Ecumenical Progress: A Decade of Change in the Ecumenical Movement, 1961–1971* (Oxford: Oxford University Press, 1979).

16. Jooseup Keum (ed.), *Together Towards Life: Mission and Evangelism in Changing Landscapes* (Geneva: WCC Publications, 2012), 2.

17. Ibid., 8.

18. John Stott (ed.), *Making Christ Known: Historic Mission Documents from the Lausanne Movement, 1974–1989* (Carlisle: Paternoster, 1996), 169.

19. Timothy Dudley-Smith, *John Stott: A Global Ministry* (Westmont, Ill.: InterVarsity Press, 2001), 125.

20. Stott (ed.), *Making Christ Known,* 169.

21. Michael Nazir-Ali, *Mission and Dialogue* (London: SPCK, 1995), 83.

22. Frederick Wilson (ed.), *Your Will Be Done: Mission in Christ's Way – The San Antonio Report* (Geneva: WCC Publications, 1990).

23. John R. Mott, *The Moslem World* (London: Hodder & Stoughton, 1925), ix–x.

24. Hendrik Kraemer, *The Christian Message in a Non-Christian World* (London: Edinburgh House Press, 1938). For a recent defence of Kraemer, see: Tim S. Perry, *Radical Difference: A Defence of Hendrik Kraemer's Theology of Religions* (Waterloo, Ont.: Wilfrid Laurier University Press, 2001).

25. Sven Ensminger, *Karl Barth's Theology as a Resource for a Christian Theology of Religions* (London: Bloomsbury, 2014); this study was supervised by one of the leading experts on inter-religious dialogue, Gavin D'Costa.

26. Wilson (ed.), *Your Will Be Done,* 26. Lesslie Newbigin said the same, and often.

27. Bradford Hinze, *Practices of Dialogue in the Roman Catholic Church* (New York: Continuum, 2006), 209, 220; Douglas Pratt, *Being Open, Being Faithful: The Journey of Interreligious Dialogue* (Geneva: WCC Publications, 2014).

28. Michael Kinnamon (ed.), *Signs of the Spirit: Official Report of the Seventh Assembly of the WCC* (Geneva: WCC Publications and Grand Rapids, Mich.: Eerdmans, 1991), 15–16.

29. Andrew Wingate, *The Meeting of Opposites: Hindus and Christians in the West* (London: SPCK, 2014), 15.

30. Stanley J. Samartha, *Courage for Dialogue: Ecumenical Issues in Inter-Faith Relationships* (Geneva: WCC Publications, 1981), 77, 139.

31. This term was likely first used by the WCC at the mission conference in San Antonio.

32. Stanley J. Samartha, *Courage for Dialogue: Ecumenical Issues in Inter-Religious Dialogue* (Geneva: WCC Publications, 1982), 139.

33. Cited in Douglas Pratt, *The Church and Other Faiths* (Bern: Peter Lang, 2010), 103–104.

34. This heading is an inversion of an article title by Leonard Swidler: "Vatican II: The Catholic Revolution from Damnation to Dialogue," *Journal of Ecumenical Studies* 50:4 (2015).

35. Jooseop Keum (ed.), *Together Towards Life: Mission and Evangelism in Changing Landscapes* (Geneva: WCC Publications, 2012), 4, 7.

36. Lesslie Newbigin, *The Ecumenical Future and the WCC: A Word in Season* (Grand Rapids, Mich.: Eerdmans, 1994), 197 (reprinted from *The Ecumenical Review* 42:1 [January 1991]).

Chapter Four: Uppsala 1968

1. John A.T. Robinson, *Honest to God* (London: SCM, 1963).

2. Norman Goodall (ed.), *The Uppsala Report 1968: Official Report of the Fourth Assembly of the WCC* (Geneva: WCC Publications, 1968), xvii.

3. Kenneth Slack, *Uppsala Report: The Story of the WCC's Fourth Assembly* (London: SCM, 1968), 9.

4. James Baldwin, "White Racism or World Community?" *The Ecumenical Review* 20:4 (1968), 371.

5. Slack, *Uppsala Report,* 31.

6. Goodall (ed.), *The Uppsala Report 1968,* 12.

7. "Report on Worship." In: Goodall (ed.), *The Uppsala Report 1968,* 78.

8. "Vatican II in Retrospect." *The Ecumenical Review* 66:4 (2014); Donald W. Norwood, *Reforming Rome: Karl Barth and Vatican II* (Grand Rapids, Mich.: Eerdmans, 2015).

9. Willem A. Visser 't Hooft, *The New Delhi Report: The Third Assembly of the WCC, 1961* (London: SCM, 1962), 6.

10. Giuseppe Alberigo and Joseph A. Komonchak (eds), *History of Vatican II,* Vol. I, 359–60 (Leuven: Peeters, 1995); Vol. II, 225–27 (Maryknoll, N.Y.: Orbis, 1998).

11. *Review and Herald: General Church Paper of the Seventh-Day Adventists* 145:32 (1968), 5.

12. Goodall (ed.), *The Uppsala Report 1968,* 117.

13. Ibid., Appendix VI, 325. Italics mine.

14. Ibid., 117.

15. Ibid., 127–29.

16. Giuseppe Alberigo and Joseph A. Komonchak (eds), *History of Vatican II,* Vol. III (Maryknoll, N.Y.: Orbis, 2000), 25, 27, 318. James Norris, a layman, was told it would be "premature" for a woman to address the Council. Norris did so in her place.

17. Roberto Tucci, S.J., in Goodall, ed., *The Uppsala Report,* Appendix VI, 323.

18. Thomas F. Best and Günther Gassmann (eds), *On the Way to Fuller Koinonia: Official Report of the Fifth World Conference on Faith and Order* (Geneva: WCC Publications, 1994), 243; para 31.2: "We recommend that the Faith and Order Commission begin a new study concerning the question of a universal ministry of Christian unity."

19. Harding Meyer and Lukas Vischer (eds), *Growth in Agreement,* Faith and Order Paper 108 (Geneva: WCC Publications and New York: Paulist Press, 1984); Jeffrey Gros, Harding Meyer and William G. Rusch (eds),

Growth in Agreement II, Faith and Order Paper 187 (Geneva: WCC Publications and Grand Rapids, Mich.: Eerdmans, 2000); Jeffrey Gros, Thomas F. Best and Lorelei Fuchs (eds), *Growth in Agreement III*, Faith and Order Paper 204 (Geneva: WCC Publications and Grand Rapids, Mich.: Eerdmans, 2007); Thomas F. Best, Lorelei F. Fuchs, SA, John Gibaut, Jeffrey Gros, FSC, Despina Prassas, eds., Growth in Agreement IV: International Dialogue Texts and Agreed Statements, 2004–2014, Books 1 and 2 (Geneva: WCC Publications, 2017).

20. Norman Tanner, SJ, *Creeds of the Ecumenical Councils* (London: Sheed and Ward and Washington, D.C.: Georgetown University Press, 1990), 58. Calvin preferred to speak of "Mother of the Son of God."

21. Goodall (ed.), *The Uppsala Report 1968,* 17.

22. Willem A. Visser 't Hooft (ed.), *First Assembly of the WCC, 1948* (London: SCM, 1949), 28–29; *The Genesis and Formation of the World Council of Churches* (Geneva: WCC Publications, 1982), 112–20.

23. Trent described itself as a "holy and general council"; Vatican I was described as "the holy ecumenical Vatican council."

24. *Councils and the Ecumenical Movement.* WCC Studies No. 5 (Geneva: WCC Publications, 1968); Hans J. Margull (ed.), *The Councils of the Church: History and Analysis* (Philadelphia: Fortress Press, 1966).

25. *Confessing the One Faith: An Ecumenical Explication of the Apostolic Faith as It Is Confessed in the Nicene-Constantinopolitan Creed (381),* Faith and Order Paper 153, (Geneva: WCC Publications, 1991).

26. Norman Tanner, SJ (English editor), *The Decrees of the Ecumenical Councils* (London: Sheed and Ward and Washington, D.C.: Georgetown University Press, 1990); *The Church in Council* (London: I. B. Taurus, 2011).

27. Lukas Vischer, "The Council as an Event in the Ecumenical Movement." In: Giuseppe Alberigo and Joseph A. Komonchak (eds), *History of Vatican II,* Vol. 5 (Leuven: Peeters, 2005), 485.

28. *Towards a Common Understanding and Vision of the World Council of Churches,* Working Draft (Geneva: WCC Publications, 1996), 31.

29. See the full document at: https://www.oikoumene.org/en/resources/documents/assembly/2006-porto-alegre/3-preparatory-and-background-documents/common-understanding-and-vision-of-the-wcc-cuv.

30. *What Unity Requires,* Faith and Order Paper 77 (Geneva: WCC Publications, 1976), 66.

31. At the Vancouver Assembly in 1983, the Eucharist was celebrated using the Lima Liturgy, compiled by Max Thurian of Taizé, expressing the agreements reached on baptism, eucharist, and ministry at Lima in 1982.

Chapter Five: Nairobi 1975

1. "In God's Hands: The Ecumenical Prayer Cycle" (Geneva: WCC, 2013).

2. David M. Paton (ed.), *Breaking Barriers, Nairobi 1975: Official Report, Fifth Assembly of the World Council of Churches* (Grand Rapids, Mich.: Eerdmans and London: SPCK, 1976), 119.

3. Betty Thompson, *A Chance to Change: Women and Men in the Church* (Geneva: WCC Publications, 1982).

4. See "The Spokeswomen." In: Susannah Herzel, *A Voice for Women* (Geneva: WCC Publications, 1981), 109–40.

5. Keith Clements, *Faith on the Frontier: A Life of J.H. Oldham* (Geneva: WCC Publications, 1999), 23–26.

6. Ibid., 203–208.

7. Josiah Ulysses Young III, *James Baldwin's Understanding of God* (New York: Palgrave Macmillan, 2014), 113.

8. David Gill (ed.), *Gathered for Life: Official Report of the Sixth Assembly of the WCC* (Geneva: WCC Publications and Grand Rapids, Mich.: Eerdmans, 1983), 151–52; Paton (ed.), *Breaking Barriers*, 109–10. Uppsala offered a definition of racism.

9. John de Gruchy, *Liberating Reformed Theology: A South African Contribution to an Ecumenical Debate* (Grand Rapids, Mich.: Eerdmans, 1991), 216.

10. John de Gruchy and Charles Villa-Vicencio (eds), *Apartheid Is a Heresy* (Cape Town: David Philip, 1983), 12.

11. Ben Marais, *Colour: The Unsolved Problem of the West* (Cape Town: Howard Jimmins, 1952).

12. Colleen Ryan, *Beyers Naudé: Pilgrimage of Faith* (Claremont, South Africa: David Philip, 2005); Charles Villa-Vicencio and John de Gruchy (eds), *Resistance and Hope: South African Essays in Honour of Beyers Naudé* (Grand Rapids, Mich.: Eerdmans, 2005).

13. Charles Villa-Vicencio (ed.), *On Reading Karl Barth in South Africa* (Grand Rapids, Mich.: Eerdmans, 1998).

14. Luis N. Rivera-Pagan (ed.), *God, in Your Grace . . .: Official Report of the Ninth Assembly of the WCC* (Geneva: WCC Publications, 2007), 303–305.

15. "Mutual accountability" is the subject of WCC general secretary Olav Fykse Tveit's doctoral thesis, published as *The Truth We Owe Each Other: Mutual Accountability in the Ecumenical Movement* (Geneva: WCC Publications, 2016).

16. Allan Boesak, *Kairos, Crisis and Global Apartheid* (London: Palgrave Macmillan, 2015), 75; *Black and Reformed* (Maryknoll, N.Y.: Orbis, 1984).

17. Barney Pityana. In: Pauline Webb (ed.), *A Long Struggle: The Involvement of the World Council of Churches in South Africa* (Geneva: WCC Publications, 1994), 92.

18. John de Gruchy, *The Church Struggle in South Africa*, 3rd ed. (London: SCM, 2004), 34.

19. Ibid., 138.

20. Alex Borraine, *A Country Unmasked* (Oxford: Oxford University Press, 2000); *A Life in Transition* (Cape Town: Zebra Press, 2008).

21. Diane Kessler (ed.), *Together on the Way: Official Report of the Eighth Assembly of the WCC* (Geneva: WCC Publications, 1999), 227–31.

22. Borraine, *A Country Unmasked*.

23. "Advance Praise" for "What Price Reconciliation?" Borraine, *A Country Unmasked*, 340–78.

24. Hugh McCullum, "Racism and Ethnicity." In: J. Briggs, M. Oduyoye and G. Tsetsis (eds), *A History of the Ecumenical Movement, Vol. Three, 1968–2000* (Geneva: WCC Publications, 2004), 347; Hugh McCullum, *The Angels Have Left Us: The Rwanda Tragedy and the Churches* (Geneva: WCC Publications, 1995); André Sibomana, *Hope for Rwanda* (London: Pluto, 1999).

25. In fairness, I should add that the Commission of the Churches on International Affairs of the WCC was very active in concern for Rwanda and offers a full account in its various published reports.

26. Konrad Raiser, in the Foreword to Pauline Webb (ed.), *A Long Struggle*, cited in McCullum, "Racism and Ethnicity," 347. See also Konrad Raiser, *The Challenge of Transformation: An Ecumenical Journey*, (Geneva: WCC Publications, 2018)

27. Roméo Dallaire, *Shake Hands with the Devil: The Failure of Humanity in Rwanda* (Toronto: Random House, 2003), 323.

28. Paton (ed.), *Breaking Barriers*, 9–21.

29. Ibid., 107, 309–10.

30. Ibid., 97–98.

31. Betty Thompson, *A Chance to Change: Women and Men in the Church* (Geneva: WCC Publications, 1982), 82.

32. Erlinda N. Senturias and Theodore A. Gill, Jr. (eds), *Encountering the God of Life: Report of the 10th Assembly of the WCC* (Geneva: WCC Publications, 2014), 28.

33. *Living Letters* (Geneva: WCC Publications, 1997).

34. The English lay theologian Dorothy Sayers (1893–1957) had written a witty essay (c.1941), "Are Women Human?" (Grand Rapids, Mich.: Eerdmans, 2005 [1971]).

35. Mercy Oduyoye, *Who Will Roll the Stone Away?: The Ecumenical Decade of Churches in Solidarity with Women* (Geneva: WCC Publications, 1990), 52.

36. *Living Letters: A Report of Visits to the Churches during the Ecumenical Decade of Churches in Solidarity with Women* (Geneva: WCC Publications,

1997), 44; "The Impact of the Decade and the Visits." In: Diane Kessler (ed.), *Together on the Way: Official Report of the Eighth Assembly of the WCC* (Geneva: WCC Publications, 1999), 43, 249.

37. Senturias and Gill, Jr. (eds), *Encountering the God of Life*, 173–76.

38. Susannah Herzel, *A Voice for Women* (Geneva: WCC Publications, 1981).

39. *Baptism, Eucharist and Ministry*, Faith and Order Paper 111 (Geneva: WCC Publications, 1982).

40. Michael Kinnamon and Michael E. Cope (eds.), *The Ecumenical Movement: An Anthology of Key Texts and Voices* (Grand Rapids, Mich.: Eerdmans, 1997), 193.

41. Hans-Ruedi Weber, *A Laboratory for Ecumenical Life: The Story of Bossey, 1946–1996* (Geneva: WCC Publications, 1996).

42. Melanie May, *Bonds of Unity: Women, Theology and the Worldwide Church* (Atlanta, Ga.: Scholar's Press, 1989).

43. Oduyoye, *Who Will Roll the Stone Away?* 57.

Chapter Six: Vancouver 1983

1. "Message from the Sixth Assembly of the WCC." In: David Gill (ed.), *Gathered for Life: Official Report of the Sixth Assembly of the WCC* (Geneva: WCC Publications and Grand Rapids, Mich.: Eerdmans, 1983), 1.

2. Ibid., 9.

3. Ibid.

4. Ibid.; *Worship Book for the Sixth Assembly* (Geneva: WCC Publications, 1983).

5. Geoffrey Wainwright, *Doxology: The Praise of God in Worship, Doctrine and Life* (New York: Oxford University Press, 1980); "When Liturgy and Ecumenism Embrace," lecture given at the Bossey Ecumenical Institute, 1993; *Worship with One Accord* (New York: Oxford University Press, 1999), 11. Edmund Schlink was an observer at Vatican II.

6. Janet Crawford, "Worship and the Search for Christian Unity." In: Thomas F. Best and Dagmar Heller (eds), *So We Believe, So We Pray: Towards Koinonia in Worship*, Faith and Order Paper 171 (Geneva: WCC Publications, 1995), 30.

7. Crawford, "Worship and the Search for Christian Unity," 30.

8. *Special Commission on Orthodox Participation in the WCC: An Introduction* (Geneva: WCC Publications, 2002).

9. Best and Heller (eds), *So We Believe, So We Pray*, 52.

10. "A Jubilee Call: A Letter to the WCC by Evangelical Participants at Harare." In: Kessler (ed.), *Together on the Way: Official Report on the Eighth Assembly of the WCC*, 266–70.

11. Constitution and Rules of the World Council of Churches (2013), Article III.

12. Emilio Castro, "Report of the General Secretary." In: Michael Kinnamon (ed.), *Signs of the Spirit: Official Report of the Seventh Assembly of the WCC* (Geneva: WCC Publications and Grand Rapids, Mich.: Eerdmans, 1991), 167.

13. Following the Ditchingham Consultation on Worship, discussions on the Eucharist took place at the Ecumenical Institute at Bossey. See: Thomas Best and Dagmar Heller (eds), *Eucharistic Worship in Ecumenical Contexts: The Lima Liturgy and Beyond* (Geneva: WCC Publications, 1998).

14. Spencer Jones (1857–1945, Rector of Batsford with Moreton-in-Marsh 1887–1932), *England and the Holy See* (London: Longmans Green and Co., 1902); *Catholic Reunion* (Oxford: Blackwell, 1930).

15. R.T. Davidson (ed.), *The Five Lambeth Conferences* (London: SPCK, 1920), 442.

16. Catherine E. Clifford, *A Century of Prayer for Christian Unity* (Grand Rapids, Mich.: Eerdmans, 2009); Mark Woodruff, *The Unity of Christians: The Vision of Paul Couturier* (London: Catholic League, 2003).

17. Willem A. Visser 't Hooft, *The New Delhi Report: The Third Assembly of the WCC, 1961* (London: SCM, 1962) 116.

18. *The Church: Towards a Common Vision*, Faith and Order Paper 214 (Geneva: WCC Publications, 2013).

19. Emilio Castro, *When We Pray Together* (Geneva: WCC Publications, 1989).

20. *Partners in Life: The Handicapped and the Church*, Faith and Order Paper 89 (Geneva: WCC Publications, 1979), 2.

Chapter Seven: Canberra 1991

1. Michael Kinnamon, "A Personal Overview and Introduction." In: Michael Kinnamon (ed.), *Signs of the Spirit: Official Report of the Seventh Assembly of the World Council of Churches* (Geneva: WCC Publications and Grand Rapids, Mich.: Eerdmans, 1991), 11.

2. Keith R. Krause (ed.), *Culture and Security: Multilateralism, Arms Control and Security Building* (New York: Routledge, 1999), 133.

3. William Temple, "Enthronement Sermon." In: *The Church Looks Forward* (London: Macmillan, 1944), 1–3.

4. *New Directions in Faith and Order, Bristol 1967*, Faith and Order Paper 50 (Geneva: WCC Publications, 1968), 25.

5. Hans Küng and Karl-Josef Kuschel (eds), *A Global Ethic* (London: SCM, 1993), 45.

6. Visser 't Hooft (ed.), *First Assembly of the WCC* (London: SCM, 1949), 89.

7. Robert McAfee Brown, "Vietnam." In: *Reflections over the Long Haul: A Memoir* (Louisville: Westminster John Knox Press, 2005), 137–82.

8. Ibid., 137.

9. Ibid., 152.

10. Fernando Enns, *Friedenskirche in der Ökumene* (Göttingen: ET, 2003); Helmut Harder, *The Peace Church and the Ecumenical Community: Ecclesiology and the Ethics of Non Violence* (Kitchener, Ont.: Pandora and Geneva: WCC Publications, 2007), xxii.

11. *Laudato Si': On Care for Our Common Home*, Encyclical Letter of Pope Francis (Vatican, 2015).

12. Larry L. Rasmussen, *Earth Community, Earth Ethics* (Geneva: WCC Publications, 1996), 189.

13. Ibid., 154.

14. Orthodox Consultation at Sofia 1987. In: Gennadios Limouris (ed.), *Justice, Peace and the Integrity of Creation: Insights from Orthodoxy* (Geneva: WCC Publications, 1990), 5, para. 47.

Chapter Eight: Harare 1998

1. Gennadios Limouris (ed.), *Orthodox Visions of Ecumenism* (Geneva: WCC Publications, 1994), 9–11.

2. Jim Forest, *The Resurrection of the Church in Albania* (Geneva: WCC Publications, 2002).

3. "Reflections of Orthodox Participants." In: Michael Kinnamon (ed.), *Signs of the Spirit: Official Report, Seventh Assembly* (Geneva: WCC Publications and Grand Rapids, Mich.: Eerdmans, 1991), 279–82.

4. "Evangelical Perspectives from Canberra." In: Kinnamon (ed.), *Signs of the Spirit*, 282–86.

5. *Special Commission on Orthodox Participation in the WCC: An Introduction* (Geneva: WCC Publications, 2002).

6. Anna Marie Aagaard and Peter Bouteneff, *Beyond the East–West Divide: The World Council of Churches and "the Orthodox Problem"* (Geneva: WCC Publications, 2002), 107. Bouteneff had been a staff member of the Faith and Order Commission.

7. Ibid., 110.

8. Metropolitan Nifon, "Challenges and Hopes for Unity: An Eastern Orthodox Perspective." In: Erlinda N. Senturias and Theodore A. Gill, Jr. (eds), *Encountering the God of Life: Report of the 10th Assembly of the World Council of Churches* (Geneva: WCC Publications, 2014), 93–96.

9. Luis N. Rivera-Pagan (ed.), *God, in Your Grace . . .: Official Report of the Ninth Assembly of the WCC* (Geneva: WCC Publications, 2007), 21.

10. Ion Bria, *The Liturgy after the Liturgy: Mission and Witness from an Orthodox Perspective* (Geneva: WCC Publications, 1996); *The Sense of Ecumenical Tradition* (Geneva: WCC Publications, 1991); *Romania: Orthodox Identity at the Crossroads of Europe* (Geneva: WCC Publications, 1995).

11. Thomas FitzGerald and Peter Bouteneff (eds), *Orthodox Reflections on the Way to Harare* (Geneva: WCC Publications, 1998).

12. "Common Understanding and Vision of the WCC: Preliminary Observations – WCC Consultation with Its Orthodox Member Churches," *The Ecumenical Review* 48:2 (1996), 185–92.

13. Metropolitan John Zizioulas, "The Self-Understanding of the Orthodox and Their Participation in the Ecumenical Movement," http://www.spc. rs/eng/selfunderstanding_orthodox_and_their_participation_ecumenical_ movement_metropolitan_john_zizioulas.

14. Jill Tabart, *Coming to Consensus: A Case Study for the Churches* (Geneva: WCC Publications, 2003).

15. Ibid., 15.

Chapter Nine: Porto Alegre 2006

1. "The Church and the International Disorder: Report of Section IV." In: Willem Visser 't Hooft (ed.), *First Assembly of the WCC* (London: SCM, 1949), 88–94. See also the four volumes written in preparation for the first assembly, especially O. Frederick Nolde, "Freedom of Religion and Related Human Rights." In: Volume 4: *The Church and the International Disorder: An Ecumenical Study Prepared under the Auspices of the World Council of Churches* (London: SCM, 1948), 143–89.

2. "Address to the Assembly by President Luiz Indicio da Silva." In: Luis N. Rivera-Pagan (ed.), *God, in Your Grace . . .: Official Report of the Ninth Assembly of the WCC* (Geneva: WCC Publications, 2007), 354–59; Charles R. Harper, *Ecumenical Action for Human Rights in Latin America, 1970–1990* (Geneva: WCC Publications, 2006).

3. Rivera-Pagan (ed.), *God, in Your Grace*, 210. Nearly a million pages of documents were kept safe in the archives of the WCC in Geneva and not made public until 2013.

4. *In Process of Formation* (Geneva: WCC Publications, YEAR).

5. M. Searle Bates, *Religious Liberty: An Inquiry* (New York: International Missionary Council, 1945), 1.

6. John Nurser, *For All Peoples and All Nations* (Geneva: WCC Publications, 2005), 28. See also Methodist theologian Esther Reed, *The Ethics of Human Rights: Contested Doctrinal and Moral Issues* (Waco, Tex.: Baylor, 2007); and Reformed theologians George Newlands, *Christ and Human Rights* (Ash-

gate: Aldershot, 2006) and Robert Traer, *Faith in Human Rights: Support in Religious Traditions for a Global Struggle* (Washington, D.C.: Georgetown University Press, 1991).

7. *The Church and the International Disorder: An Ecumenical Study Prepared under the Auspices of the World Council of Churches* (London: SCM, 1948).

8. Nurser, *For All Peoples and All Nations*, 29.

9. Though the Constitution separates church and state, to date no one would ever be elected who was not a Christian, and with the one exception of Kennedy, a Protestant.

10. Mary Ann Glendon, *A World Made New: Eleanor Roosevelt and the Universal Declaration of Human Rights* (New York: Random House, 2001); Johannes Morsink, *Universal Declaration of Human Rights: Origin, Drafting and Intent* (Philadelphia: University of Pennsylvania Press, 1999).

11. Heather Warren, *Theologians of a New World Order* (New York: Oxford University Press, 1997); Scott M. Thomas, *The Global Resurgence of Religion and the Transformation of International Relations* (New York: Palgrave Macmillan, 2005).

12. Kenneth Grubb, *Crypts of Power: An Autobiography* (London: Hodder and Stoughton, 1971), 163–200.

13. Johannes Morsink, *Universal Declaration of Human Rights: Origin, Drafting and Intent* (Philadelphia: University of Pennsylvania Press, 2000).

14. "International Affairs: Christians in the Struggle for World Community." In: Willem A. Visser 't Hooft (ed.), *The Evanston Report: The Second Assembly of the World Council of Churches* (London: SCM, 1954), 130–51, especially paragraphs 27, 37, 45, 51.

15. Robert McAfee Brown, *Reflections over the Long Haul: A Memoir* (Louisville: Westminster John Knox Press, 2005).

16. Pope Paul VI, *Dignitatis Humanae* (Declaration on Religious Freedom) (Vatican, 1965), 2.

17. Ibid., 1.

18. Julio R. Asensio, "The Situation of Evangelical Churches in Spain." In: Thomas F. Best and Günther Gassmann (eds), *On the Way to Fuller Koinonia: Official Report of the Fifth World Conference on Faith and Order* (Geneva: WCC Publications, 1994), 210–12.

19. Rivera-Pagan (ed.), *God, in Your Grace*, 265–73.

20. Thomas K. Johnson (ed.), *Global Declarations: On Freedom of Religion or Beliefs and Human Rights* (Eugene, Ore.: Wipf and Stock, 2017), 85.

21. "Resolution on the Rights of the Aboriginal Peoples of Canada," in David Gill, ed., *Gathered for Life: Official Report, VI Assembly* (Geneva: WCC Publications, 1983), 164.

22. David Gill (ed.), *Gathered for Life: The Official Report of the Sixth Assembly of the World Council of Churches* (Geneva: WCC Publications, 1983), 164.

23. David M. Paton (ed.), *Breaking Barriers, Nairobi 1975: The Official Report of the Fifth Assembly of the World Council of Churches* (Geneva: WCC Publications, 1976), 102, 131, 178.

24. "Statement on Torture," *The Ecumenical Review* 29:4 (1977), 406–408.

25. Gill (ed.), *Gathered for Life*, 88, 139, 152.

26. George Hunsinger (ed.), *Torture Is a Moral Issue* (Grand Rapids, Mich.: Eerdmans, 2008).

27. Ibid., 81.

28. George Hunsinger, *Conversational Theology* (London: Bloomsbury, 2015), 165–77, 175.

29. "A Letter to the Assembly from the US Conference of WCC Member Churches." In: Rivera-Pagan (ed.), *God, in Your Grace*, 360–61.

30. Rivera-Pagan, *God, in Your Grace*, 195–96.

31. Gillian Paterson, *Love in a Time of AIDS* (Geneva: WCC Publications, 1996); *Facing AIDS: The Challenges. The Churches' Response. A Study Document* (Geneva: WCC Publications, 1997); Ezra Chitando, *Living with Hope: African Churches and HIV/AIDS* (Geneva: WCC Publications, 2007); Gillian Paterson (ed.), *Dignity, Freedom and Grace* (Geneva: WCC Publications, 2016).

32. *Together on the Way: Official Report of the Eighth Assembly*, 8.7a. A Jubilee Call: A Letter to the WCC by Evangelical Participants at Harare (Geneva: WCC Publications, 1999).

33. Donald Messer, *Breaking the Conspiracy of Silence* (Minneapolis: Fortress, 2004).

34. WCC AIDS Working Group, *Learning about AIDS: A Manual for Pastors and Teachers* (Geneva: World Council of Churches/Christian Medical Commission, 1989).

Chapter Ten: Busan 2013

1. *The Ecumenical Review* 66:2; 66:3 (2014).

2. *The Ecumenical Review* 66:3 (2014), 384.

3. Luis N. Rivera-Pagan (ed.), *God, in Your Grace . . .: Official Report of the Ninth Assembly of the WCC* (Geneva: WCC Publications, 2007), 11–12.

4. Ernst Lange, *And Yet It Moves: Dream and Reality of the Ecumenical Movement* (trans. Edwin Robertson) (Grand Rapids, Mich.: Eerdmans, 1979), 147.

5. Annemarie Mayer, "Toward the Difficult Whole: 'Unity' – A Woman's Perspective," *The Ecumenical Review* 64:3 (2012), 314–27.

6. Pope Paul VI, *Gaudium et Spes* (Pastoral Constitution on the Church in the Modern World) (Vatican, 1965), 1.

7. "Message of the Ninth Assembly." In: Rivera-Pagan (ed.), *God, in Your Grace*, 35–36.

8. "Report of the Programme Guidelines Committee." In: Rivera-Pagan (ed.), *God, in Your Grace*, 244.

9. Michael Kinnamon, *Can a Renewal Movement Be Renewed? Questions for the Future of Ecumenism* (Grand Rapids, Mich.: Eerdmans, 2014), 4.

10. Ibid., 153.

11. Olav Fykse Tveit, "Unity: A Call to Be Strong or Humble," *The Ecumenical Review* 65:2 (2013), 170–81.

12. *Moral Discernment in the Churches: A Study Document*, Faith and Order Paper 215 (Geneva: WCC Publications, 2013); "Ecumenical Dialogue on Moral Issues." In Jeffrey Gros, Harding Meyer and William G. Rusch (eds). *Growth in Agreement II*, Faith and Order Paper 187 (Geneva: WCC Publications and Grand Rapids, Mich.: Eerdmans, 2000), 900–10; Michael Root and James J. Buckley (eds), *The Morally Divided Body: Ethical Disagreement and the Disunity of the Church* (Eugene, Ore.: Cascade, 2012).

13. Olav Fykse Tveit, "Mutual Accountability." In: *That They All May Be One: Selected Sermons, Speeches and Articles*, presented to the WCC central committee (Geneva: WCC Publications, 2011), 66; *The Truth We Owe Each Other: Mutual Accountability in the Ecumenical Movement* (Geneva: WCC Publications, 2016).

14. Olav Fykse Tveit, "People and Communities of Faith Living with HIV," speech from Amsterdam, 22–23 March, 2010, available at: https://www.oikoumene.org/en/resources/documents/general-secretary/speeches/religious-leadership-in-response-to-hiv.

15. Constitution and Rules of the World Council of Churches (2013), Article III.

16. Simon Oxley, "Getting Nowhere," *The Ecumenical Review* 63:2 (2011), 153–59; Unpublished thesis.

17. "Final Report: Continuation Committee on Ecumenism in the 21st Century," *The Ecumenical Review* 60:3 (2008).

18. Johannes Brosseder and Hans-Georg Link (eds), *Eucharistische Gastfreundschaft* (Neukirchener, 2003).

19. Dietrich Werner et al. (eds), *Handbook of Theological Education in World Christianity* (Oxford: Regnum Books, 2010); Dietrich Werner and Isabel Phiri (eds), *Theological Education in Africa* (Oxford: Regnum Books, 2013).

20. Paulo Freire and Antonio Faundez, *Learning to Question: A Pedagogy of Liberation* (trans. Tony Coates) (Geneva: WCC Publications, 1989). Faundez, from Chile, also served as a consultant to the WCC.

21. *The Church for Others: A Quest for Structures for Missionary Congregations* (Geneva: WCC Publications, 1968).

22. Charles Villa-Vicencio, *A Theology of Reconstruction* (Cambridge University Press, 1992).

23. See Diane Kessler, "Harare 1998: An Introduction and Personal Perspective," 1.13, in idem, ed., *Together on the Way: Official Report of the Eighth Assembly of the World Council of Churches* (Geneva: WCC Publications, 1999).

24. Ibid., 103, 23-24, 153, 168.

25. Huibert van Beek (ed.), *Revisioning Christian Unity: The Global Christian Forum* (Oxford: Regnum Books, 2009); Brian Woolnough, *The Global Christian Forum, 1998–2007 and Beyond* (Oxford: Oxford Centre for Mission Studies, 2008); Richard Howell (ed.), *Global Christian Forum: Transforming Ecumenism* (New Delhi: Evangelical Fellowship of India, 2007).

26. Comments on the most recent Forum are drawn from articles in *Transformation* 30:4 (2013).

27. Nils Ehrenstrom and Walter G. Muelder, *Institutionalism and Church Unity* (London: SCM, 1963); "Institutionalism and Church Unity." In: *Old and New in the Church*, Faith and Order Study 84 (London: SCM, 1960), 52–91.

28. Kessler (ed.), *Together on the Way*, 154.

29. Ibid., 168–70, 169.

30. Noel Davies and Martin Conway (eds), *World Christianity in the Twentieth Century: SCM Reader* (London: SCM, 2008), 83.

31. Rivera-Pagan (ed.), *God, in Your Grace*, 171–74.

32. Walter Brueggemann, *Hopeful Imagination* (London: SCM, 1992), part 3.

33. *Living Letters: A Report of Visits to the Churches during the Ecumenical Decade of Churches in Solidarity with Women* (Geneva: WCC Publications, 1997), 11; Mercy Oduyoye, *Who Will Roll the Stone Away? The Decade of Churches in Solidarity with Women* (Geneva: WCC Publications, 1990).

World Council of Churches
TIMELINE

1st Assembly, Amsterdam 1948

Place: Amsterdam, The Netherlands
Dates: 22 August to 4 September 1948
Theme: **Man's Disorder and God's Design**
Member churches: 147

It was on the 23rd of August 1948, in
Amsterdam, that the World Council of
Churches was officially founded. One hundred and forty-seven
churches from different confessions and many countries came
together to commit themselves to the ecumenical movement.

At the assembly in Amsterdam, four sections were organized to
examine aspects of the theme "Man's Disorder and God's Design":

- The universal church in God's design
- The church's witness to God's design
- The church and the disorder of society
- The church and the international disorder

2nd Assembly, Evanston 1954

Place: Evanston, Illinois, USA
Dates: 15–31 August 1954
Theme: **Christ – the Hope of the World**
Member churches: 161

The only WCC assembly to date held in the United States, it to some degree reflected – and certainly reflected on – the East–West tensions of the Cold War. The assembly divided its work into six sections:

- Our oneness in Christ and our disunity as churches
- The mission of the church to those outside her life
- The responsible society in a world perspective
- Christians in the struggle for world community
- The churches amid racial and ethnic tension
- The laity: the Christian in his vocation

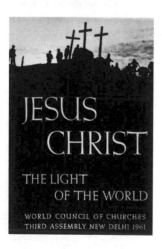

3rd Assembly, New Delhi 1961

Place: New Delhi, India
Dates: 19 November to 5 December 1961
Theme: **Jesus Christ, the Light of the World**
Member churches: 197

Best remembered for the incorporation of the International Missionary Council into the WCC, and the admission of 23 new member churches, including significant sectors of Eastern Orthodoxy and churches from newly independent nations, the assembly focused on the theme "Jesus Christ, the Light of the World" with three sections on witness, service and unity.

4th Assembly, Uppsala 1968

Place: Uppsala, Sweden
Dates: 4–20 July 1968
Theme: **Behold, I Make All Things New**
Member churches: 235

The assembly at Uppsala bore further testimony to the expanding membership of the WCC, as well as the fresh breezes of Vatican II that brought Catholic observers to participate in the meeting and discuss further opportunities for cooperation. Sections were organized under the headings:

- The Holy Spirit and the catholicity of the church
- Renewal in mission
- World economic and social development
- Towards justice and peace in international affairs
- Worship
- Towards new styles of living

5th Assembly, Nairobi 1975

Place: Nairobi, Kenya
Dates: 23 November to 10 December 1975
Theme: **Jesus Christ Frees and Unites**
Member churches: 285

"Jesus Christ frees and unites," the delegates sang in the midst of Nairobi's life: people from around the earth, standing before God in their captivities and disunities and naming a divine possibility.

The assembly section titles echo concerns of that turbulent decade:

- Confessing Christ today
- What unity requires
- Seeking community
- Education for liberation and community
- Structures of injustice and struggles for liberation
- Human development

6th Assembly, Vancouver 1983

Place: Vancouver, British Columbia, Canada

Dates: 24 July to 10 August 1983

Theme: **Jesus Christ, the Life of the World**

Member churches: 301

At this assembly on the western shores of
Canada, a renewed emphasis on common
worship was experienced under the great
white tent standing beneath the summer
sun. Hope for closer fellowship arose from
dialogue on the B*aptism, Eucharist and Ministry* (BEM) document, and such ecumenical experiments as
the Lima Liturgy. At the same time, the nuclear threat and neo-
colonialism glowered like dark clouds on the horizon. The assembly proclaimed its theme: "Jesus Christ, the Life of the World,"
and carried out its work in the following issue groups:

- Witnessing in a divided world
- Taking steps towards unity
- Moving towards participation
- Healing and sharing life in community
- Confronting threats to peace and survival
- Struggling for justice and human dignity
- Learning in community
- Communicating credibly

7th Assembly, Canberra 1991

Place: Canberra, Australia
Dates: 7–20 February 1991
Theme: **Come, Holy Spirit, Renew the Whole Creation**
Member churches: 317

The 1991 assembly was the first time a theme had explicitly invoked the third person of the Trinity, and it did so in the context of the physical universe. Sections were organized under four sub-themes:

- "Giver of life – sustain your creation!"
- "Spirit of truth – set us free!"
- "Spirit of unity – reconcile your people!"
- "Holy Spirit – transform and sanctify us!"

8th Assembly, Harare 1998

Place: Harare, Zimbabwe
Dates: 3–14 December 1998
Theme: **Turn to God, Rejoice in Hope**
Member churches: 339

Half a century after the official foundation
of the WCC, its member churches renewed
their commitment to stay together, and
delegates promised to remain in solidarity
with their African hosts.

The assembly decided to set up a commission on the participation
of the Orthodox churches in the WCC. It backed the creation of
a "Forum of Christian Churches and Ecumenical Organizations"
which could extend the ecumenical outreach far beyond WCC
member churches.

Delegates and assembly visitors participated in more than 600
contributions to a three-day "Padare" in which subjects ranged
from Evangelical–Orthodox dialogue to human sexuality.
It was preceded by a Decade Festival of Churches in Solidarity
with Women.

God, in your grace,
transform the world

World Council of Churches
9th Assembly
14-23 February 2006
Porto Alegre, Brazil

9th Assembly, Porto Alegre 2006

Place: Porto Alegre, Brazil
Dates: 14–23 February 2006
Theme: **God in Your Grace, Transform the World**
Member churches: 348

The 2006 assembly was one of the most representative gatherings of Christians ever held – with over 4,000 participants from ecumenical organizations and groups, delegates from 348 member churches, observers, and visitors from all around the world.

Addressing the core issues of Christian unity, the assembly agreed on a new text, "Called to be the One Church," and urged that WCC and its member churches give priority to the questions of unity, catholicity, baptism, and prayer. Other key issues discussed at plenary sessions were "Economic justice," "Christian identity and religious plurality," and "Youth overcoming violence."

Also, delegates adopted a substantially revised Constitution and Rules which moved the WCC to decision making based on consensus and which amended membership criteria. Steps were taken to strengthen active involvement of youth (under 30 years) in the life and work of the WCC.

10th Assembly, Busan 2013

Place: Busan, Republic of Korea
Dates: 30 October–8 November 2013
Theme: **God of Life, Lead Us to Justice and Peace**
Member churches: 345

In the message of the 2013 assembly at Busan, participants offered this affirmation:

"We share our experience of the search for unity in Korea as a sign of hope in the world. This is not the only land where people live divided, in poverty and richness, happiness and violence, welfare and war. We are not allowed to close our eyes to harsh realities or to rest our hands from God's transforming work. As a fellowship, the World Council of Churches stands in solidarity with the people and the churches in the Korean peninsula, and with all who strive for justice and peace.